Women's Roles & Gender Differences In Development

SEX ROLES in the NIGERIAN TIV FARM HOUSEHOLD

by
Mary E Burfisher
Nadine R. Horenstein

Cases for Planners

SEX ROLES in the NIGERIAN TIV FARM HOUSEHOLD

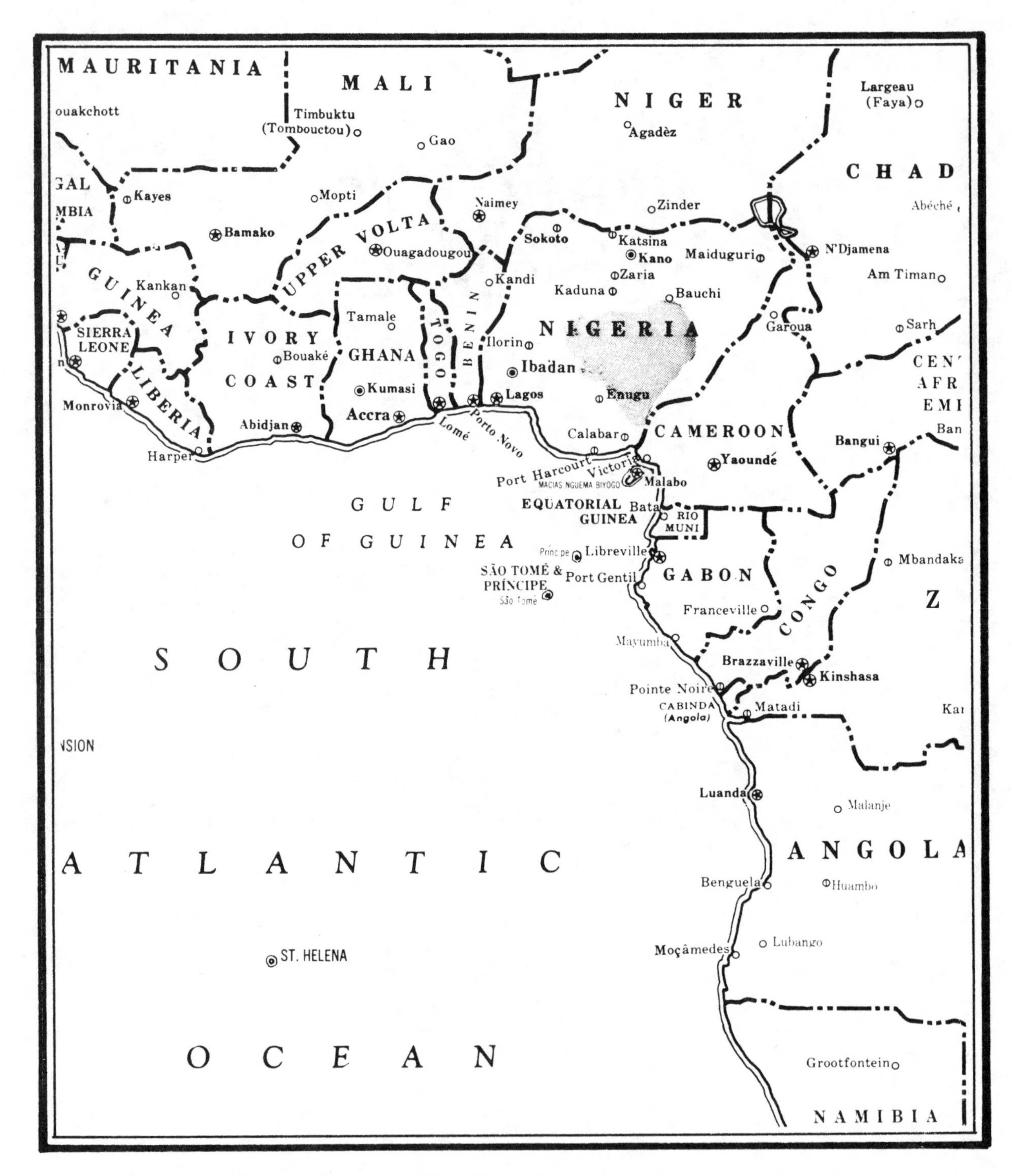

The Project Area

Women's Roles & Gender Differences In Development

SEX ROLES in the NIGERIAN TIV FARM HOUSEHOLD

Mary E. Burfisher
Nadine R. Horenstein

KUMARIAN PRESS
West Hartford

Printed in the United States of America

Cover design by

Timothy J. Gothers

Library of Congress Cataloging in Publication Data
Burfisher. Mary E.
Sex Roles in the Nigerian Tiv farm household.
Bibliography: p. 59.
1. Tivi (African people)—Economic conditions.
2. Women, Tivi (African people) 3. Agriculture—Economic aspects—Nigeria. 4. Rural development—Nigeria. 5. Sexual division of labor—Nigeria.
I. Horenstein, Nadine R., 1954- . II. Title.
DT515.45.T58B87 1985 331.4'83'089963 84-28547

ISBN:0-931816-17-3

KUMARIAN PRESS
29 Bishop Road
West Hartford, CT 06119

CONTENTS

LIST OF ILLUSTRATIONS

ACKNOWLEDGMENTS

The authors wish to thank the people who provided valuable insights and needed encouragement. We thank especially Judith Bruce, Abe Weisblat, and Donna Vogt for the time they took to comment on our ideas and follow our progress. In addition, we are grateful for the written comments of Kate Cloud, Nancy Hafkin, Richard Longhurst, Ingrid Palmer, Emmy Simmons, Melinda Smale, Dunstan Spencer, Kathleen Staudt, Leslie Whitener and Donald Vermeer. We want to thank Liz Davis for her statistical assistance and Cheryl Christensen and the Africa and Middle East Branch. Also, our special appreciation to Deloris Midgette, Victoria Valentine and Denise Morton for their help and patience in typing our study.

PREFACE

Why should development planners and scholars of development be concerned about women's roles and gender differences?

No project that expresses its goals in terms of production gains or increased benefits can afford to ignore the economic potential and needs of one-half of the population. Guidelines for the design and evaluation of development projects sensitive to women's roles have often been applied only to a narrow range of "women's projects." Our view at the Population Council is that all development efforts could be improved if the differential impact on both class and gender groupings were considered.

The series of case studies on Women's Roles and Gender Differences in Development was developed to demonstrate that such analyses are not only essential, but also feasible within existing structures.

These case studies make clear how inattention to women's roles and gender differences is played out as projects are implemented. Excluding gender as a variable, or limiting women's roles to the welfare sector, results in unintended effects, sometimes positive, but more frequently negative. Many of the stated objectives of the development schemes under study were not attained because project designs were predicated on an incomplete picture of the society to be served and drawn into participation.

The case studies draw largely from material that existed originally in other forms (such as exceptional Ph.D dissertations). From these materials has been extracted the "case:" (1) salient aspects of the culture and society in which the development project was placed, (2) the project dynamics themselves, and finally, (3) an assessment of gains and losses in different goal areas. To complement individual case studies, the Series for Planners includes monographs on broader development phenomena whose effects are seen outside the confines of specific development schemes. As of this writing, the Series includes two monographs, one dealing with the effects of male out-migration on rural women's roles and a second on the impact of different styles of agrarian reform on women's roles and productivity.

These materials are intended to be used by students of development and professionals in the field, including those at the highest planning levels. By providing examples of how individual development schemes have operated vis-a-vis gender, we hope they stimulate in the reader an interest in exploring what these effects might be in development projects being designed, implemented, or evaluated. For some time now, an understanding of class dynamics has been seen as essential in designing projects for successful outcomes. We have the same conviction regarding the importance of understanding gender differentials. We hope that this study series positively advances that notion and provides its readers with new skills and insights by raising questions and suggesting alternatives.

We wish to thank each of our individual authors for the exhaustive work they have put into forming their material into case studies. We commend Marilyn Kohn for her fine editorial work in finalizing the material.

Judith Bruce
Associate
The Population Council

Ingrid Palmer
Editor of the Series

SUMMARY

PURPOSE OF STUDY

This paper provides a planning methodology that takes into account sex role differences in the farming household. It examines the expected impact of a development project which was designed with the assumption of an aggregate or corporate household. It then compares this expected impact to the impact which might be expected using the proposed planning methodology in which project impacts are disaggregated by sex.

The study focuses on the division of labor, income and financial obligations among one ethnic group in the project area--the Tiv--and the implications of these divisions for the ability and incentives of each sex to adopt technologies introduced by the agricultural development project. In the analysis, ethnographic information on sex roles in the farm household is used to disaggregate the intended impact of the project on the total farm into the impact on each sex in order to test two hypotheses:

> The amount and seasonality of female and male labor requirements are affected differently by project interventions because of their different labor roles regarding crops and tasks by crop.
>
> Women's and men's income levels and income-earning opportunities are affected differently by project interventions because of their different sources of income and different household expenditure responsibilities.

BACKGROUND

There are several reasons why sex role differences are particularly relevant within the context of Sub-Saharan agriculture. First, a variety of studies indicates that the chief constraint on agricultural production in this region is labor availability at critical times of the year. Labor bottlenecks manifest themselves during peak farming periods when several operations such as planting, ridging, thinning and weeding must be performed simultaneously. Labor availability to meet these peak requirements places a limit on the amount of land that a family can farm and also on the ability of a farm household to adopt labor-increasing technologies.

These problems relating to the availability and seasonality of farm labor can be exacerbated by sex role differences. In most areas of Sub-Saharan Africa, cultural traditions have created a sharp sexual division of labor in the household. Men and women typically control different crops and carry out different tasks; for example, women might do all the weeding and men might do all the field preparation. In addition, studies have shown sometimes substantial differences in the amount of time spent by each sex on farm and household labor, suggesting some rigidity in the household pooling of family labor across different tasks in order to meet total labor requirements. Thus, sex roles relating to labor in the farm may lead to project outcomes different from those anticipated by conventional planning, which uses the total farm as the unit of analysis.

Second, in addition to their different labor roles, women and men in the African farming household typically have different sources of income and different financial responsibilities. Women's and men's sources of assets and income are generally linked to their different obligations and labor roles, with each sex earning and controlling income from different crops and activities. Women are frequently responsible for their own and their children's food and clothing, and women's contribution to their families' nutrition may be crucial at certain times of year. Men's earnings frequently go toward large farming and family expenses and toward their own personal expenses.

For instance, among the Tiv of Nigeria, a woman earns and controls income from yams, a crop for which she performs most of the labor. A woman uses yams to feed her family, and she then uses the proceeds from the sale of surplus yams to meet other responsibilities for household expenses. Men earn and control income from millet and rice, crops which are used for home consumption but which are also important marketed crops.

Different sources of income and financial responsibilities can mean a lack of incentive for one sex to contribute labor to crop production that financially benefits the other sex. Different returns to labor for each sex can also exacerbate labor bottlenecks in the face of conflict over labor allocations. For example, where women are typically responsible for producing food crops for home consumption, they may be less interested than men in increasing their labor in cash crop production, which is frequently a male income-earning activity. In general, the sources of income for each sex have an important influence on the extent to which increased labor will be made available for competing farm activities, suggesting that if the different incentives of each sex are not calculated, the project may have different results than would have been expected on the basis of conventional analysis.

Finally, a growing body of research has documented that, while there is much variation, women have important roles in food production in Sub-Saharan Africa, and in some areas they are the primary producers. Women are estimated to perform 60 to 80 percent of all agricultural work and to provide up to 70 percent of the region's food. In Nigeria, which provides the setting for this study, women have historically had important roles in food processing and petty trading. They have also contributed to food production and this role is now increasing, with male migration to urban areas considered to be a crucial factor in this regard.

Even in the northern Muslim areas of Nigeria, where a woman's movement outside the home is circumscribed by the practice of wife seclusion, women have been discovered to play a central role in the region's economy through a "hidden" trade in food, processed by women in their homes and sold at competitive prices by market intermediaries, usually their own children. Women in this area also have a significant but generally unrecognized role as hired farm laborers.

In Nigeria, as in most of Sub-Saharan Africa, the significance of women's roles in agriculture and the sharp differences between male and female roles suggest that efforts to increase farm production and productivity need to give explicit attention to both female and male farmers. In particular, if one role of development projects is to identify and remove key bottlenecks to the more efficient use of resources, much may be missed if more detailed, within-household analyses are not done.

METHODOLOGY

In this study, farming systems research methodologies are used to understand both the internal structure of the farm household and the wider farm context in order to analyze how women and men are affected differently by project interventions. Determination of differential project impacts is made by linking new labor requirements with current labor roles for each sex and changes in income with the sources of income and the nature of financial responsibilities for each sex. This analysis permits an assessment of the differential project impacts on each sex, and of the potential constraints in the adoption of new technologies and cultural methods because of sex role differences.

OBJECTIVES OF THE PROJECT

The project is intended to improve agricultural productivity and increase farm incomes in Nigeria's "middle belt," which forms an important food producing reserve for the nation. The project's central activities relate to the development of nine major crops. The project plans to improve yields, thus increasing both local food supplies for domestic consumption and the marketable surplus to generate additional income. It also targets development of the area's livestock, forestry and fisheries sectors. As an integrated development project, it provides for comprehensive development of roads, water supplies, training programs, and commercial services in order to provide farmers with the necessary training, inputs and credit for effective project participation.

FINDINGS

Labor requirements: On the typical 2.5 hectare farm, total labor requirements were expected to increase by 14 percent annually. When female and male requirements were disaggregated, it was found that there were significant differences and that women would carry a disproportionate share of this increase. Female labor requirements on the typical farm were expected to increase by 17 percent, as compared to an expected 6 percent increase for men. This is due to the fact that women have primary responsibility for harvest, post-harvest and storage activities, and the project increases production by improving yields rather than expanding acreage. Furthermore, the different roles of women and men results in contrasting labor profiles. The project interventions result in a major shift in women's labor profile, indicating potential bottlenecks at different times of year. Men's labor profile shifts only slightly, in accordance with the favorable shift anticipated using aggregated data (see Table 2; Charts 1-6).

Income: Net returns per person and per hectare are estimated from single crop budgets using projected farm-gate prices for inputs and outputs and projected yields. Based on the total farm, net returns were expected to increase by 31 percent. Disaggregating by sex, the analysis finds that women's returns are also expected to increase by 31 percent, while men's increase by 28 percent. The changes in total earnings, however, mask some important asymmetries between increased labor and increased income for each sex on some crops. The disaggregation by sex of the change in daily net returns provides a measurement of the incentive of each sex to contribute labor to a particular crop. Women have a central role in controlling food crops; thus they control more of the increases in production, or returns, from the project than men. It is important to note, however, that the actual cash component of net returns will most likely be much smaller than the in-kind component. Men's net returns may have a greater cash component due to their greater responsibility for crops which are marketed (See Tables 3 and 4).

Implications of the non-corporate household: Because of the sex role differences in the Tiv farming household, a development project cannot depend upon pooled family labor as a resource or on shared family income as an incentive for the adoption of new technologies. The different roles of each sex cause them to have different constraints and flexibilities and thus causes the project to affect them differently. Some of the major implications are:

The effect of increasing women's labor disproportionately to men's may impair the ability of women to meet new labor requirements, and reduce the productivity of women relative to men in the family household.

Many activities of the farm household such as water hauling, cooking, and food processing are not addressed by the project.

While both sexes in this project have the potential for increased incomes from those crops which are marketed, increased labor requirements are not always associated with increased income.

Non-financial incentives such as women's responsibilities for family nutrition and the need for leisure time also play a crucial role in determining if, and to what extent, new technologies are adopted by members of the farm household.

ALTERNATIVES FOR PROJECT DESIGN

At the project design stage, there is a need for sex-disaggregated socio-economic baseline data. This would facilitate the analysis of work patterns, labor requirements, and financial interactions and obligations within the household. If the household is viewed as an integrated production and consumption unit, then all relevant activities of the household members can be taken into account, without making the often misleading distinction between farm and non-farm activities. If this framework were applied to the project, these alternative project designs might be suggested:

A home economics program which includes processing and storage techniques could do much to counterbalance the increased labor component for women caused by the project. (Although according to project documents there are provisional plans to establish an itinerant home economics team in the project's fifth year, the delay in starting this program and its provisional nature is an indication that the project is not emphasizing some important farm household needs, particularly those farm activities not undertaken by men.) To the extent that processing and storage of non-project crops may create a bottleneck for women in November and December, improving their efficiency in these tasks could ease another important constraint to their adoption of project technologies. In addition, developing food processing technologies could develop, or improve, the potential for the sale of processed food as a source of cash income for women farmers.

There is also a need for the project to underscore the outreach of extension services to women farmers. This is a very typical area in which projects fail to serve women. Project interventions are more likely to be adopted by both female and male farmers if the primary agent of change, the extension service, is targeted toward them both.

Future plans, which include residential training and building, forestry, and road-building activities, should recognize the role of women and thereby maximize the impact of interventions.

Improvement of marketing channels should take into account the need to provide both sexes' crops with market development assistance, and the project should consider that price and marketing conditions in the project area may cause differential access to income from marketed crops.

The local political structure, which is used by the project as a communication channel with local people, does not provide equal representation for women and men. The project should ensure that women have direct access to project personnel and do not have to rely on men for communication of their interests. This might be done by including any existing women's organizations on the local project committee.

Other factors which could be considered in order to maximize the impact of the project are:

Women's access to land as affected by the land tenure system and population growth and migration;

Education and its potential impact on child labor and hence on women; also, educational efforts should attempt to reach both sexes;

Farm credit availability. (At this point credit is not available to either sex in any significant manner. However, women's lack of direct land holding rights and their lack of direct political access have the potential for weakening their credit worthiness if credit develops in the future.)

CONCLUSION

Distinguishing between women's and men's roles, and considering the implications of these role differences, is crucial to the process of improving productivity and income. Too long perceived as a social welfare issue, the concept of women's role in development needs to be perceived for what it is: an important productivity issue that should be a standard part of the planning process. If one goal of development is ultimately the integration of both women and men, then the different needs and incentives of each must be explicitly recognized and addressed so that projects and program can become responsive to the people they are designed to assist.

BACKGROUND TO THE STUDY

INTRODUCTION

Declining per capita food production in many areas of Sub-Saharan Africa during the past two decades has led to a closer examination of traditional farming systems and of the factors that may be impeding efforts to improve agricultural productivity. One of the factors which is beginning to receive increased attention on a theoretical level is sex role differences in the farming household and their effects on the allocation of household resources. On an operational level, however, few development projects explicitly take this factor into consideration. Instead, projects whose objectives include increasing farm productivity and income are designed using the aggregated labor and income resources of the farming household as a basis for analysis, and assuming a corporate household entity as decision-maker in the allocation of household resources.

This paper provides a planning methodology that takes into account sex role differences in the farming household. It also provides a quantitative comparison between the project impacts of a development project using a conventional planning methodology based on the aggregated farm household, and the proposed methodology, in which project impacts are disaggregated by sex.

The study uses data from the planning documents of an actual project in central Nigeria. However, since the purpose of this study is to provide a framework for studying sex role differences in the farm household, and not to evaluate the outcome of a specific project, the project will remain unidentified. The project's goals are to increase agricultural productivity and improve farm family incomes. It includes a basic technological package of improved inputs and new or improved cultivation methods. It also provides for a variety of other services such as training, extension, and water, road, and forestry development. The project bases its analysis of project outcomes on a hypothetical 2.5 hectare farm on which a combination of early, full season, and late crops are grown.

The study focuses on the divisions of labor, income and financial obligations among one ethnic group in the project area--the Tiv--and the implications of these divisions for the ability and incentives of each sex to adopt technologies introduced by the agricultural development project.

In the analysis, ethnographic information on sex roles in the farm household is used to disaggregate the intended impact of the project on the total farm into the impact on each sex in order to test two hypotheses:

> The amount and seasonality of female and male labor requirements are affected differently by project interventions because of their different labor roles regarding crops and tasks by crop.
>
> Women's and men's income levels and income-earning opportunities are affected differently by project interventions because of their different sources of income and different household expenditure responsibilities.

The analysis is carried out without changing the project's assumptions concerning adoption rates, yields and prices. However, the homogeneity and non-differentiation of household resources are called into question throughout the analysis.

The analysis suggests that gender specific roles and responsibilities may result in different responses to production-increasing technologies because of the different constraints and incentives of each sex. These sex role differences may cause development projects to have unintended effects or to face constraints not anticipated by conventional project analyses based on the total farm resources. Thus, projects may fail to reach their objectives. Project planning that takes sex role differences into account can help in designing projects that are more responsive to the different needs and interests of both women and men farmers.

THE LAND AND THE PEOPLE

There are several reasons why sex role differences are particularly relevant within the context of Sub-Saharan agriculture. First, a variety of studies indicate that the chief constraint on agricultural production in this region is labor availability at critical times of year. [1] Labor bottle- necks manifest themselves during peak farming periods when several operations such as planting, ridging, thinning and weeding must be performed simultaneously. Labor availability to meet these peak requirements places a limit on the amount of land that a family can farm and also on the ability of a farm household to adopt labor-increasing technologies.

These problems relating to the availability a[illegible] seasonality of farm labor can be exacerbated by sex rol[illegible] differences. In most areas of Sub-Saharan Africa, cultural traditions have created a sharp sexual division of labor in the household. [2] Men and women typically control different crops and carry out different tasks, such as women doing all weeding and men doing all field preparation. In addition, studies have shown sometimes substantial differences in the amount of time spent by each sex on farm and household labor, suggesting some rigidity in the household pooling of family labor across different tasks in order to meet total labor requirements. [3] These labor role differences may lead to project outcomes different from those anticipated by conventional planning which uses the total farm as a unit of analysis.

Second, in addition to their different labor roles, women and men in the African farming household typically have different sources of assets and income and different financial responsibilities. Women's and men's sources of assets and income are generally linked to their different obligations and labor roles, with each sex earning and controlling income from different crops or activities. Women are frequently responsible for their own and their children's food and clothing, and women's contribution to their families' nutrition may be crucial at certain times of the year. [4] Men's earnings frequently go toward large farming and family expenses and toward their own personal expenses. [5]

For instance, among the Tiv of Nigeria, a woman earns and controls income from yams, a crop for which she performs most of the labor. A woman uses yams to feed her family, and uses proceeds from the sale of surplus yams to meet other responsibilities for household expenses. Men earn and control income from millet and rice, crops which are used for home consumption but which are also important marketed crops.

Different sources of income and financial responsibilities can mean a lack of incentive for one sex to contribute labor to crop production that financially benefits the other sex. Different returns to labor for each sex can also exacerbate labor bottlenecks in the face of conflict over labor allocations. [6] For example, where women are typically responsible for producing food crops for home consumption, they may be less interested than men in increasing their labor in cash crop production, which is frequently a male income-earning activity. In general, the sources of income for each sex have an important influence on the extent to which increased labor will be made available for competing farm activities, suggesting that if the different incentives of each sex are not calculated, the project may have different results than would have been expected on the basis of conventional analysis.

Finally, a growing body of research has documented that, while there is much variation, in general women have important roles in food production in Sub-Saharan Africa, and in some areas they are the primary producers. Women are estimated to perform 60 to 80 percent of all agricultural work and to provide up to 70 percent of the region's food. In Nigeria, which provides the setting for this study, women have historically had important roles in food processing and petty trading. They have also contributed to food production and this role is now increasing, with male migration to urban areas considered a crucial factor in the growing farming responsibilities of Nigerian women. [7]

Even in the northern Muslim areas of Nigeria where women's movement outside the home is circumscribed by the practice of wife seclusion, women have been discovered to play a central role in the region's economy through a "hidden" trade of food, processed by the women in their homes and sold at competitive prices by market intermediaries, usually their own children. [8] Women in this area also have a significant but generally unrecognized role as hired farm laborers. [9]

In Nigeria, as in most of Sub-Saharan Africa, the significance of women's roles in agriculture and the sharp differences between male and female roles suggest that efforts to increase farm production and productivity need to give explicit attention to both female and male farmers. In particular, if one role of development projects is to identify and remove key bottlenecks to the more efficient use of scarce resources, much may be missed if more detailed, within-household analyses are not done.

The rest of Part I provides an overview of the Tiv farm and environment including the operations of the farm, land and credit resources, the marketing system, the local political system, and the sex roles in the Tiv farm household. It goes on to describe activities planned by the project, and then discusses the methodology of the study and sources of data. Part II provides an analysis of the data, and examines implications for project design. A brief summary and conclusions of the study are presented in Part III.

THE TIV FARM AND ENVIRONMENT

The Tiv Farm Household

The Tiv are an agricultural people who farm the savannah lands to the north and south of the Benue River in central Nigeria. They comprise about one-half of the population of 500,000 included in this agricultural development project, which is being implemented north of the Benue River, about 140 kilometers east of its confluence with the Niger River.

The Tiv live in scattered, isolated compounds throughout the project area that are bound together by strong family ties and physically linked by the myriad of paths that criss-cross the countryside. The compounds are each made up of between three and forty huts with the average composed of about ten huts.

The number of people living in a compound also varies considerably, with the average having approximately 17 members. The people living in the compound form an extended patrilineal polygamous family consisting of a compound head, his wife or wives, their children, unmarried adult daughters, adult sons and their wives and children.

The size of the farm reflects the number of agriculturally active people in the compound. In theory, the compound head has control over the size and location of the fields of each person in the compound. In practice, however, discussion of allocation of fields takes place among all the adult males of the household. All compound members have a right to sufficient land to meet their food and financial obligations; these rights are protected by traditional sanctions. Tiv women and men both hold major roles in crop production activities, and women are active in food processing and trading. Children assist parents in farm tasks and carry much of the responsibility for early child care, thus freeing adult women for other kinds of work. In 1976, Nigeria introduced Universal Primary Education, which is expected to provide free primary school education to all children. The project area, however, is located in one of Nigeria's most educationally disadvantaged states. Child labor is therefore likely to still be an important component of the Tiv's farm labor resources.

The ranking of co-wives and the age of household members are among the factors that affect one's status within the household. However, information on these role differences is extremely limited.

The Farm System

The Tiv have a reputation for being excellent farmers. They produce a wide variety of crops using flexible systems of undersowing, relay cropping and intercropping. Crops are produced on two kinds of farms: bush farms located at a distance from the family compound, and compound farms, or kitchen gardens, immediately surrounding the family compound. On the bush farms, farming follows a bush/fallow cycle with a four to six year crop cycle and a five to ten year fallow period. Yam, the principle crop grown by the Tiv, is the first crop in the cycle. It is followed by millet and sorghum.

Cassava is the last crop in the cycle, and if cassava yields are considered high a second crop might be planted before the field goes into fallow. Occasionally a second yam crop is planted following the sorghum rotation if the soil fertility is adequate. These yams are then staked on the sorghum stalks left standing in the field for that purpose.

The Tiv practice intercropping; crops that are commonly intercropped on the bush farm are melons, groundnuts, bambara nuts and benniseed. However, principle crops are usually grown sole or as a single dominant crop and the various admixtures have an insignificant effect on crop yields.

The compound farms benefit from household waste and ash disposal so that they remain fertile enough to support continuous crop production. A wide variety of crops are planted in the compound farm. It is usually rotated between maize and sorghum but also produces such crops as cocoyam, tomato, pepper, okra, pumpkin, sorrel, peanuts, cowpeas and various other vegetables. These crops are given great care, occasionally receiving hand watering until the onset of the rainy season.

There is little livestock production on the Tiv farm because of the presence of the tsetse fly in this region. However, some small stock such as chickens, pigs, and goats are raised as scavengers around the compound to provide meat for home consumption.

Other income activities of the farming household include processing and trading of agricultural products, spinning and weaving, and pottery making.

Farm Resources: Land and Credit

The Tiv are for the most part subsistence farmers. Thus, in addition to labor, which is discussed in Chapter Two, farm resources are limited to land and some seasonal needs for capital. Farming is undertaken almost entirely by hand, and the scarcity of hired help limits farm size.

The land tenure system of the Tiv is typical of many patrilineal groups in Sub-Saharan Africa. Every adult Tiv male has a right, by virtue of his membership in a compound group, to enough land to provide each of his wives with a farm. Every married Tiv woman has a right to a farm of sufficient size to feed herself, her children, and her husband. A husband is allotted land to allocate to his wives by the compound head.

As the Tiv population increases, the need for land also increases. It is the responsibility of the head of the compound to control enough land to support the compound. He does this by expanding fields outward against the land of the neighbor who is most distantly related to him. This concentric expansion creates a great deal of local friction.

A Tiv woman's rights to land are dependent upon her relationship to a husband. A woman has land rights only when she is married and living with a man, although a widow continues to have land rights if she remains resident in her husband's compound. Unmarried women have no land rights. They work on their mother's fields or may be allocated small fields by their brothers. Although national law relating to women's land rights is changing to provide them with more security, the customary land tenure systems prevail.

Small holder farm credit remains a difficult problem in Nigeria. Commercial banking is not well developed; in 1981 the country had fewer than 800 branches for a total population of over 80 million. Commercial banking services in rural areas are particularly poor. Even where banks are ready to supply credit, few farmers are able to offer adequate security for the loans they need to improve their farms and their productivity. In turn, farmers with little security are reluctant to take out credit. Generally, few farmers have access to the limited commercial credit that is available; most depend on local or traditional sources for their seasonal credit needs.

Little information is available on credit sources among the Tiv. However, traditional associations for men and women are widespread in rural Nigeria. One such association used by women is a contribution club or esusu whose aim is to assist its members in small-scale capital formation.

Women who join these clubs contribute small amounts at regular intervals to the pool of funds. Members then have access on a rotating basis to the money pool for investment or profit-making purposes. These associations may exist in the Tiv area, although no specific information is available.

Prices and Marketing

Tiv farm production is composed entirely of food crops; some of it is marketed and a large proportion is used for home consumption. Since 1977, several of the food crops have been covered by Nigeria's expanded marketing board system. Under the system, farmers can sell their produce either to marketing boards at floor producer prices or to local traders and consumers. There are currently seven marketing boards, each with responsibilities for handling specific food or export crops. In 1980, official producer prices for millet increased by 81 percent, sorghum by 73 percent, corn by 35 percent and rice by 24 percent.

It is estimated, however, that throughout Nigeria only about 10 percent of most food crops are marketed. Road conditions are so poor that it is difficult for most farmers to transport produce to the market. Much of it must be headloaded for long distances on bush paths.

In the area in which the Tiv live, most of the produce that is marketed is traded in a large number of local, unconnected markets. Prices can vary substantially between markets. Because food storage capacity is limited, and characterized by high losses, much of the farm produce is marketed at harvest time. Thus, there are also pronounced seasonal price movements within markets.

Local Political Structures

The political organization of the Tiv is unusual in its degree of decentralization and egalitarianism. The basic unit is the compound, made up of an extended patriarchy. The compound head is usually the oldest male of his generation. He has responsibility for deciding all matters of importance concerning the family, including the allocation of fields to male compound members who in turn assign fields to their wives.

Above the compound is a kindred composed of several compounds, or extended family groups. The authority in the kindred is an elected elder or elders, usually the head of a compound, with both political and spiritual responsibilities. An elder is usually an older man, who is judged to have the qualities necessary for peace-keeping among the Tiv because of his personality, ability, and knowledge.

The affairs of several kindreds are governed by a council of elders, consisting of a democratic council of all family group elders. This council meets extensively to discuss all problems of concern to the community. Only agnatic male members of the lineage may become elders of the council. Women are excluded because they are believed to lack the necessary spiritual qualities.

Women can exercise informal power within the compound because of their control over the food supply. They hold a great deal of authority in domestic affairs. However, they lack direct access to and a means to participate in recognized political structures.

Division of Labor on Staple Crops

Tiv women and men both have major roles in crop production activities, and these roles are sharply differentiated by sex. While few farming activities are carried out solely by women or men, there is a definite sense of which tasks are appropriate to each sex, and few tasks are performed by both men and women. Grass pulling to clear new fields is one of the few examples of a task performed by both sexes, but even here men will stop pulling grasses as soon as enough field is cleared for them to switch to mound building in preparation for planting yams.

Much of the work on the farm's staple crops is done by both men and women, with each performing different but generally complementary tasks. For example, preparation of rice fields involves hand weeding of the fields by the women and construction of trenches and ridges by men. Harvesting of rice, millet and sorghum is done jointly by women and men, with men cutting the stalks, women cutting off and bundling the heads of grains, and men transporting the bundles to the compound. In the case of yams, both sexes may be responsible for planting (although it is mostly done by women) but each does it in a different way. Women drop the seed yam into a hole made with their digging stick while men maneuver the seed yam into place with a short handled hoe.

Two major tasks in the farming household, women's weeding and men's preparation of mounds and ridges, are carried out by each sex for all crops, regardless of who controls the disposition of the crop. In general, however, the total labor input into a crop is related to control over its disposition. Yams provide the clearest example of this. Once yam mounds are built, women handle all other responsibilities for yam production, harvesting, and processing, and they control the disposition of the crop between household consumption and its sale in the market. They also control any income from its sale.

In Table 1, the labor roles of male and female farmers in the production of the nine crops targeted by the project are presented. From the table it can be seen that Tiv women have a dominant labor role for yams, sorghum, cowpeas and maize. These are important subsistence crops in this region, and yams are also important as a marketed crop. Men provide more labor than women on millet and melons which are both home-consumed and marketed. Both sexes contribute about equally to rice, cassava and benniseed, which are also important as both food crops and as marketed crops.

The figures in Table 1 represent the proportion provided by each sex of the total time required for each of the tasks associated with a crop. The proportions assigned to each sex are estimates based on the available ethnographic literature, which are applied to data provided by project documents on the number of person days required for each task. Some of the categories of activities used by the project lump together a number of component activities. Of these "lumped" categories, field preparation includes clearing land, any weeding that must be done prior to planting, and construction of mounds or ridges for some crops. Harvesting includes harvesting activities in the field and transportation of the crop back to the compound. Processing varies by crop, and includes such activities as threshing, drying and shelling.

Female and Male Income Sources and Responsibilities

In a semi-subsistence economy where much of what is produced is consumed on the farm, income must be more broadly defined to include not only cash income, but also income in the form of agricultural produce or other physical goods and services. It is clear, therefore, that not only cash income, but also the enchange of goods and services within the farm household is an important component of income.

Among the Tiv, within-household exchange reflects the Tiv's values of the communal responsibility to share, as well as payment in kind for the performance of specific tasks. For example, women frequently receive millet from men to process and sell on their own account in return for their labor input on men's fields. Similarly, men usually receive some variable quantity of yams from women's fields in return for the participation in clearing yam fields.

TABLE I: FEMALE AND MALE LABOR CONTRIBUTIONS TO, AND INCOME FROM, STAPLE CROPS.

CROP	Field Preparation	Planting	Weeding	Harvesting	Processing	Storage	Income
Yam	F: 50% M: 50%	F: 80% M: 20%	F	F	F	F	F: 80% M: 20%
Millet	M	F: 20%	F	F: 50%	F	F: 50%	F: 20% 3
Sorghum	M	F: 20% M: 80%	F	F: 50% M: 50%	F	F	F
Cassava	F: 25% M: 75%	F: 75% M: 25%	F	F: 75% M: 25%	F	F	F: 75% 2 M: 25%
Maize	F: 25% M: 75%	F: 90% M: 10%	F	F: 90% M: 10%	F	F	F
Rice	F: 10% M: 90%	F	F	F: 50% M: 50%	F: 50% M: 50%	F	F: 20% M: 80%
Benniseed	M	F: 50% M: 50%	F	F: 50% M: 50%	F	F	F: 40% 3 M: 60%
Water melon	F: 25% M: 75%	F: 25% M: 75%	F	F: 25% M: 75%	F	F	F: 25% 3 M: 75%
Cowpeas	F: 25%	F	F	F	F	F	F

1 Income refers to the value of the total crop, both the marketed and home-consumed proportions, valued at market prices projected by the project.

2 Women produce and control most of the cassava, but men are beginning to produce and sell some amounts

3 Men control most of the income from the crop although women produce small amounts for home consumption or sale.

In certain cases there are also more formal monetary relationships between members of the household. Foodstuffs can be sold within the household; for example, a woman may buy millet or sorghum from her husband to make beer, or a woman can sell cassava for her husband and make a profit. Also, loans are made between spouses, frequently with interest attached. However, the liquid assets or income of the total household are not an adequate measure of the household's capacity or incentive to respond to new opportunities, such as those presented by an agricultural development project, since surpluses from these resources are not as mobile between sexes as planners usually suppose. See Appendix III for information on net returns by crop.

Intra-household financial and exchange relationships can be quite complex. The giving of an unspecified part of one's crop to the other sex in exchange for labor input, and the arrangement of loans between spouses at various rates of interest suggest how difficult it is to quantify these relationships, or concepts such as total income or returns to labor on a subsistence or semi-subsistence farm.

In this analysis, we use ethnographic material on the Tiv to postulate a plausible division of income within the household (see Table 1). The division reflects the value of the proportion of each crop over which each sex has control. This control stems from the disposition of the crop between home consumption and sale, and the use of the crop or income from it to meet obligation toward household support. In the case of yams, for example, women are estimated to control 80 percent of the yam crop and to give 20 percent to men for men's use in entertaining and ceremonies. Women thus earn 80 percent of the value of the yam crop while men earn 20 percent, but women's and men's returns per day of labor input into the crop can differ because of their different labor roles.

Within Tiv society, a woman owns the produce which is grown on the farm allocated to her by her husband and controls the disposition of her crop between sale and home consumption. While this allocation continues, she determines the use made of this land. Tiv women are responsible for producing, and thus they control, the major portion of the Tiv's subsistence food. They derive income from sales of surplus produce, either in its natural state or in processed form, and use this income to help provide for themselves and their families, in accordance with their obligations.

Yams are considered to belong to women and are in the effective control of the senior wives or mothers-in-law. A man can request surplus yams from his wives for gift or for sale since he contributed to their production by hoeing the mounds. A woman also has a right to all the seed yams produced on her farm and can sell those which are not needed for next year's crop.

Sorghum is also controlled by women, although it is planted by men, as are all side crops which are intercropped in women's yam field or grown in kitchen gardens. These side crops are used in sauces and are an essential nutritive component of the family diet. Some sorghum is traded locally in the form of grain, or it is processed into beer and sold. Women control all the cassava grown in their yam fields and can earn income by selling the surplus at the market. Since cassava is not a valued dietary staple among the Tiv, much of it tends to be marketed. As cassava has become more important as a cash crop, men have begun to grow more of it on their own fields. Women may sell cassava given to them by the men and receive a portion of the profit. In colonial times benniseeds were as important cash crop and proceeds were used by men to pay taxes. More recently, rice has become an important cash crop and men have taken increasing responsibility for its production.

Men have primary responsibilities for millet although women may be entitled to a portion of the crop in return for their labor input in weeding and harvesting. Women also grow small quantities of millet with their yams, and derive income from brewing and selling millet beer. The millet controlled by women may also be a surplus after the family has been fed or that which is purchased in small amounts from other women.

Women can also earn money from trade in a large variety of side crops (sauce trade) or in food prepared from these crops. Trading is considered a woman's task, and thus women sell not only those crops produced on their fields but also at least a portion of the output from men's fields. Men also spend considerable time hunting during the dry season.

Each sex's sources of income are linked with responsibilities toward family support. In Tiv society, women have primary control over the crops used to provide the family's food. Their responsibility to feed the family either directly from produce from their own fields or from their husband's fields or indirectly through the sale and purchase of crops stems from this control. With income earned through petty trading women have the responsibility to provide clothing for themselves and their children. They also purchase items such as soap and other household items with their earnings.

Men have specific responsibilities toward their wives, including allocating fields, clearing land, hoeing yam mounds, and providing seed yams for each wife's first yam crop. In addition men control millet, rice, and some cassava. They also earn income from weaving and fishing, and contribute to family food supply through their hunting.

It should be noted that status within the family is an important determinant of duties and income. A compound head, a husband, or a senior wife has specific responsibilities which flow from his or her status within the community and the family. Age also affects status within the household.

In this study we do not disaggregate the impacts of the project among individuals of the same sex because of the scarcity of information.

PROJECT ACTIVITIES

The project is intended to improve agricultural productivity and increase farm incomes in Nigeria's "middle belt" which forms an important food producing reserve for the nation. The project's central activities relate to the development of the area's crop production. The project plans to improve yields of nine major crops, thus increasing both local food supplies for domestic consumption and the marketable surplus to generate additional income. It also targets development of the area's livestock, forestry and fisheries sectors. As an integrated development project, it provides for a comprehensive development of roads, water supplies, training programs, and commercial services to ensure effective project participation.

The Project Area

The project covers 9,400 square kilometers in north-central Nigeria, 140 kilometers east of the confluence of the Niger and Benue Rivers. The project area is characterized by a gently undulating topography bounded on three sides by major rivers: Mada in the west, Dep in the east and Benue in the South. The rivers are bordered by extensive flood plains.

Rainfall is about 1,200 millimeters annually. It occurs during the long wet season from March to October, which is followed by an intense dry season with dust-bearing harmattan winds from November to March. Soils in the area are of low to moderate fertility. They cannot sustain cropping for long periods and recuperate slowly during fallow. Soils in the project area have been declining in fertility because population growth and inflation create pressures to intensify production.

Communal forests cover over 32,000 hectares; however, uncontrolled cutting and subsequent extensive weed growth is downgrading wood production and quality. About 70 percent of the population in Nigeria depends on fuelwood as their primary source of cooking and heating energy. Wood supply in the project area has been in short supply since the 1930s, and government forestry efforts have not been very effective.

The population in the project area is ethnically diverse, with over 20 tribal communities. Besides the Tiv, major groups are Alago, Kanari, Eggon, Migili and Fulani. Almost half the population are Tiv, who live in small, isolated hamlets linked by strong family ties. Most of the other ethnic groups live in large concentrated villages.

There has been steady immigration to the area since the civil war. Total population growth between 1973 and 1980 is estimated at 4 percent per year. In 1980, the population was estimated at about 500,000. Eighty percent of the population is engaged in agriculture, with about 60,000 farm families averaging 6 to 7 members cultivating 150,000 hectares.

Services and communication in the area are not well developed. Education and medical facilities are rudimentary. In 1976, about 6,000 students, or three percent of the population, were in primary school. The area has one hospital and two health centers. Water supplies are generally inadequate with only the state capital having a piped water supply and electricity. The rural population relies on seasonal, and often contaminated, streams and wells. Communications in the area are by road and small river transport, and road conditions are poor.

Farmers' services are minimal, and remain almost entirely in the hands of the public sector. Supply of inputs by the Government or private traders is limited. Effectiveness of the small extension staff is severely hampered by lack of resources. Credit is available only from traditional sources.

The project area is administered by two Local Government Councils. Local authority is vested in traditional headmen and chiefs who act as arbitrators in minor disputes, organize community undertakings and generally attend to local needs. The traditional authority is widely respected and exerts considerable influence on all sections of the community.

Crop Development

The central project interventions are the improved farming practices and technologies relating to crop production. Farmer's yields are expected to increase through the introduction of a basic service package (BSP) of improved seeds, seed dressings, fertilizers and insecticides, supported by a more intensive and better trained extension service.

Although recognizing that farmers grow a whole range of crops with annually changing proportions, the project uses a hypothetical 2.5 hectare farm with a typical cropping pattern for the area, as the basis for its analysis of changes in labor requirements and income levels. The crops targeted by the project are the major crops grown in this area: yams, cassava, sorghum, millet, maize, melon, rice, cowpeas, and benniseed.

It is expected that varying proportions of each crop will continue to be cultivated under traditional methods. Overall, some 32 percent of the cropped area is expected to benefit from new or improved cultivation practices.

Labor availability to meet peak labor requirements is recognized as a key constraint to expanding production in the project area. The new cultivation practices introduced by the project increase the annual labor requirement of the hypothetical 2.5 hectare farm by 14 percent but they are planned so as to take account of potential labor bottlenecks that could develop during peak farming periods when many tasks have to be performed at once. This is to be done by encouraging a slight decrease in early season crop planting which make high demands on labor during peak farming months but offer low returns. See Appendix I for labor requirements of individual crops.

This shift is expected to distribute the increased labor demands of the project interventions throughout the year rather than in the peak months of June through September. The increased volumes of production are expected to lead to increased family income, in terms of both increased home consumption and increased marketed surplus.

Traditionally, most inputs have been procured, distributed and sold through the private sector. Fertilizer has been a state government responsibility and it is sold at heavily subsidized prices. However, procurement has been sporadic and its limited availability has led to an active black market trade. The project expects to improve distribution and availability of inputs by establishing 209 Farm Service Centers (FSC), located to achieve an optimum balance between access and delivery of supplies to hinterlands which, in Tiv areas, may be up to 150 kilometers from the nearest road.

Credit

Since fertilizer is heavily subsidized, seasonal credit is not expected to be a prerequisite to achieving the anticipated adoption rates for improved practices. Input sales are to be made on a cash basis and short-term financial requirements are expected to be met from local sources. An important proportion of this credit is found at the family level.

Services

The condition of the road network is critical to successful delivery of inputs and the evacuation of produce. The extent of the road network in the project area is considered adequate. However, the condition of the roads is poor and they are frequently impassable during the rainy season. The project is expected to undertake both improvement of existing roads and construction of new roads. Because of the importance of roads to the project's success, road maintenance activities are expected to begin at the start of the project.

The project will attempt to make potable water available to all rural families. Most small hamlets, in which the Tiv live, are situated near perennial streams, and the most pressing water supply problems are in the medium and large villages. The local government councils currently have a well construction and maintenance program. Project activities would integrate and expand the well program.

In support of these activities, the project provides for extension and training programs for farmers.

Market Development

Despite the significantly greater volume of production expected as a result of inputs, and new or improved cultivation practices, the project assumes that crop prices are not expected to decline because of rising food demand from Nigeria's urban population. The increased production is expected to be readily absorbed into the economy with no significant impact on local market prices.

ANALYTIC FRAMEWORK AND METHODOLOGY

The activities of a farming household and the operations of a development project take place within a complex social, political and economic environment. The nature and dynamics of this environment have an important influence on the technical relationship between the farming household and the project, and consequently on the ability of the project to achieve its objectives.

The farming systems research methodologies are useful in understanding the operations of the small farm within its wider context. It reflects a holistic perspective of the whole farm/ rural household and the technical and human environment. The objective of these methodologies is to understand the farming unit as an integrated production and consumption unit and to understand the constraints and flexibilities of the farmers as they try to reach their goals.

In this study, farming systems methodologies are used to understand both the internal structure of the farm household and the wider farm context in order to analyze how women and men are affected differently by project interventions. In particular, the analysis focuses on sex role differences within the household with regard to labor roles, sources of income, and financial responsibilities. These differences can give rise to a within-household pattern of constraints and flexibilities different from that of a corporate unit under one management voice and with perfect mobility of resources. It can also result in different relationships between them and such factors as credit availability and local political representation. These, too, can contribute to differential impacts of a project.

Schematic Framework

In order to apply elements of the farming systems approach to our analysis of project/farmer interactions, we developed a schematic framework. The framework identifies variables relating to the farming household, the development project, and the wider farm context that influences the project intervention process. The framework is intended to focus on the different roles of women and men in the farming household and on the differences between the interactions of women and men with the project and the farm context. Specifically, the framework is used to highlight changes in total labor requirements, in labor requirements by crop activity, and in returns to labor (income) by crop and crop activity.

DIAGRAM I: SCHEMATIC FRAMEWORK

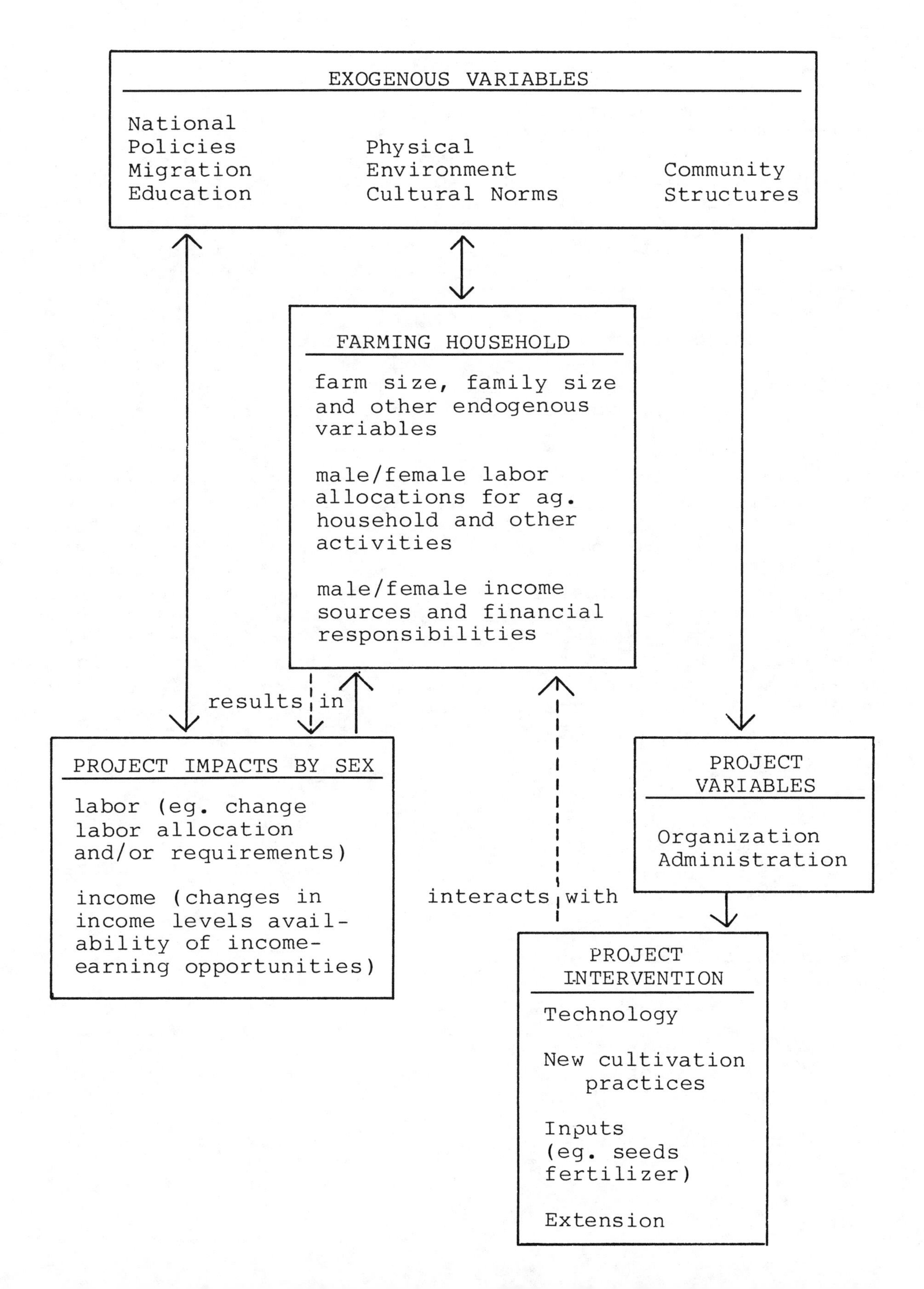

Exogenous variables are those that may be influenced but not controlled by the development project. These include: national policies, particularly those relating to prices, marketing and distribution; migration, which alters the composition and functioning of the household; education/training which has implications for the ability to have access to, or utilize, project information, as well as for the availability of household labor; the physical environment, which determines crop mix, planting strategies, and applicability of new technologies; cultural norms, which define appropriate roles and responsibilities for the household members; and community structures which establish hierarchies and systematic ways for community members to live and work together. All of these variables have an impact, to a greater or lesser degree, on: the organization and administration of a project, the structure and functioning of the farming household and the final impact of the agricultural project. In turn, the changes effected by the project can feed back and affect the exogenous variables. For example, increased income opportunities in the project area can lead to reduced out-migration or even in-migration.

Project variables include project organization and administration. Project organization includes representation of the interests of women and men on the project staff and in decision-making positions within any local groups and organizations that may be utilized by the project for management, communication of interests or concerns, and decision-making. Project administration includes consideration of how project services are delivered; for instance, whether residential training is likely to be feasible for a woman with daily household responsibilities, and whether credit is dependent upon land as collateral or issued for only certain kinds of farm operations.

The way the project is organized and administered determines how and to whom the project's interventions are delivered. In this case study, the project interventions are: improved crop varieties and cultivation practices, fertilizer, training and extension, and infrastructural development.

Method of Analysis and Data Sources

In this study, determination of differential project impacts is made by linking new labor requirements with current labor roles for each sex, and changes in income with the sources of income and the nature of financial responsibilities for each sex.

Data on labor requirements of the hypothetical total

farm for the crops being affected by the project were provided by project documents. This included farm labor requirements in person days, by month and by crop activity (such as planting, weeding, etc.), from before and after the project. The project documents also provided information on net returns from each of the crops being affected by the project, from before and after the project. Although some portion of each crop is consumed on the farm, the project documents measure income as the value of the total crop, at present and projected prices, whether it is consumed at home or marketed.

Information on the appropriate sex role for each task is drawn from the field research of Paul and Laura Bohannan, Donald Vermeer, and others. Data was collected from the early 1950s through the mid-1970s. In combining ethnographic data and information in project documents, it appears that little change has occurred during this period in the farming practices of the Tiv in this sparsely populated area, although population pressures to the south of the project area have resulted in a modification of the Tiv's crop rotation practices. In the project area, crop mixtures, cropping methods, the use of simple tools, limited marketing of produce and little out-migration indicate little change in the fundamental structure of the farm household. In the future, however, continued in-migration could eventually contribute to population pressure in this area, too.

In the analysis, the ethnographic information on the farm household was combined with the data on labor requirements provided by project documents. In some cases, however, categories of activities used by the project had the drawback of lumping together in one category many different kinds of component tasks and in some cases combining in one category distinctive female and male contributions. In order to maintain the distinction between female and male labor inputs, a proportion of each activity had to be assigned to each sex in some cases. These proportions are based on an understanding of the cropping cycle, appropriate sex roles, and the component tasks of a farming activity, with the assumption that these proportions will not change. Necessarily, however, the proportions are approximations, and data results must be interpreted in that light. These assessments are discussed more fully in Appendix II.

FINDINGS: ANALYSIS AND IMPLICATIONS OF THE DIFFERENTIAL IMPACTS OF THE PROJECT

CHANGES IN LABOR REQUIREMENTS

One of the primary objectives of the agricultural development project is to increase farm productivity and the production of major crops. The introduction of improved technical production packages is expected to significantly increase yields and output levels. As a consequence of these technical developments, the annual labor requirement of the hypothetical 2.5 hectare farm will increase by fourteen percent (see Table 2). Much of this labor increase is concentrated in harvest and storage activities, with significant increases in post-harvest and land preparation.

The relatively large increases in labor requirements for harvesting and storage reflect the fact that the project increases production by improving yields rather than expanding acreage. Consequently, labor requirements for land preparation and planting do not increase as much as labor requirements for handling the increased volume of production.

Since women have the major role in harvest, post-harvest and storage activities, they carry a disproportionate share of the increase in the farm's total annual labor requirement. Over the year, their total labor input on a typical farm will increase by 17 percent compared to a 6 percent increase for men.

Just as critical as changes in total labor requirements are the changes in seasonal labor requirements for each sex. Because women and men have different labor roles, their farm labor profiles, which indicate labor requirements for each month of the year, are different from each other's profiles and from that of the total farm. Consequently, labor bottlenecks appear at different times for each sex, indicating different patterns of flexibilities and constraints in female and male labor availability.

In the project area, labor peaks for the total farm prior to the project occurred in June, July, and August, with continued high labor requirements during September to December. January through May was a relatively slack period for labor on the project crops (see Chart 1). The effect of the changed labor requirements as a result of the project is to even out the total farm labor profile throughout the year. This is accomplished by slightly decreasing labor requirements during the previously off-peak months of April,

May, and September through December (see Chart 2).

Prior to the project, women's peak months corresponded with the peak months of the total farm (see Chart 3). As for the total farm, the effect of project activities on women's labor requirements is to decrease June's peak labor requirements and increase labor requirements for non-peak months. However, the dominance of women's roles in the activities for which labor is most increased by the project (harvesting, post-harvest and storage) results in very great increases of 35 to 50 percent in their labor during October through December. Except for August, November and December become women's new peak labor months. Labor requirements in these two months surpass even the labor required during the peak weeding period, which is usually considered to be women's most time-consuming farming activity see (Chart 4). In addition, women's labor requirements in two months, August and December, surpass the number of days in those months. This could be mitigated, however, by the presence of several women in a polygamous household.

TABLE II: CHANGES IN LABOR REQUIREMENTS BY ACTIVITY FOR MEN, WOMEN, AND THE TOTAL FARM

ACTIVITY	Change in labor requirement for women	Change in labor requirement for men	Change in labor requirement for total farm
Preparation	11	-4	0
Planting	5	0	4
Weeding	2	N.A.	2
Harvesting	37	6	26
Post-harvest	11	-35	22
Storage	41	-12	37
Fertilizing	N.A.	2	2
Staking	1	N.A.	1
Spraying	N.A.	3	3
Total	17	6	14

N.A.= not applicable

1 Staking is a new activity, accounting for one percent of women's total labor, post-project.

2 Fertilizing is a new activity, accounting for seven percent of men's total labor, post-project. We make the assumption that this new activity will be undertaken by men.

3 Spraying is a new activity, accounting for one percent of men's total labor, post-project. We make the assumption that spraying will be undertaken by men.

Source: Based on Bohannan and Bohannan, Vermeer and Project Documents

CHART 1

TOTAL FARM LABOR PROFILE (PRE-PROJECT)

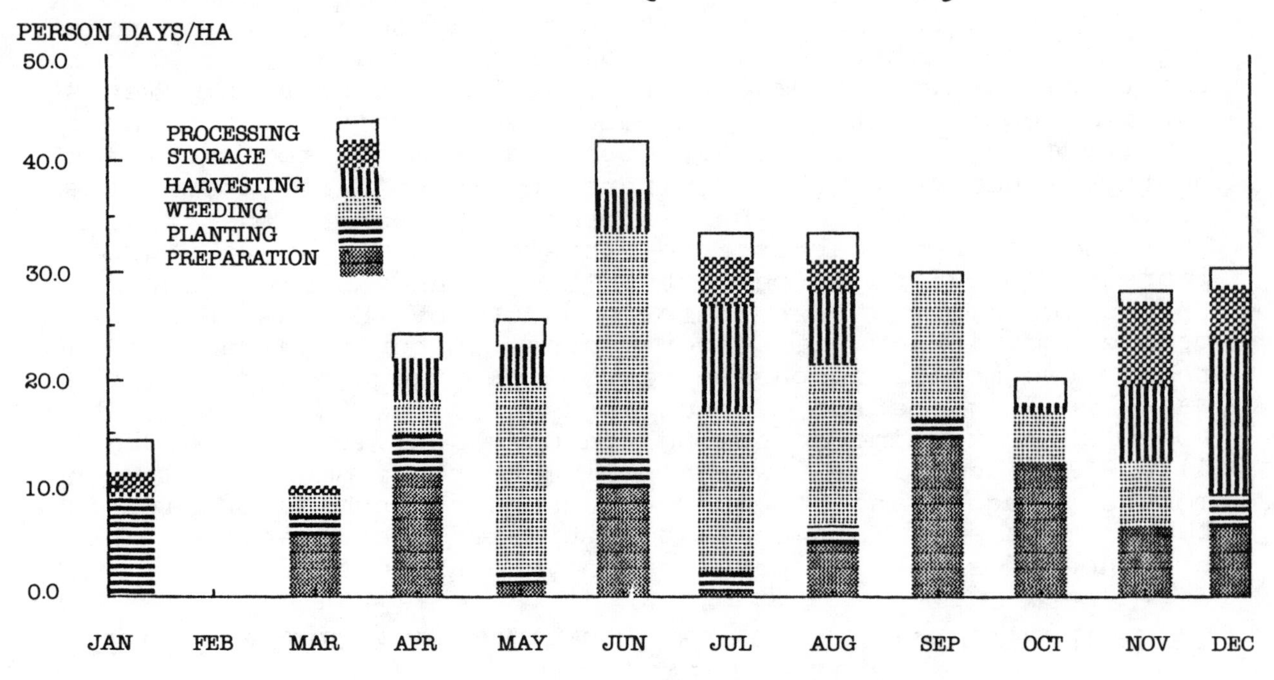

CHART 2

TOTAL FARM LABOR PROFILE (POST-PROJECT)

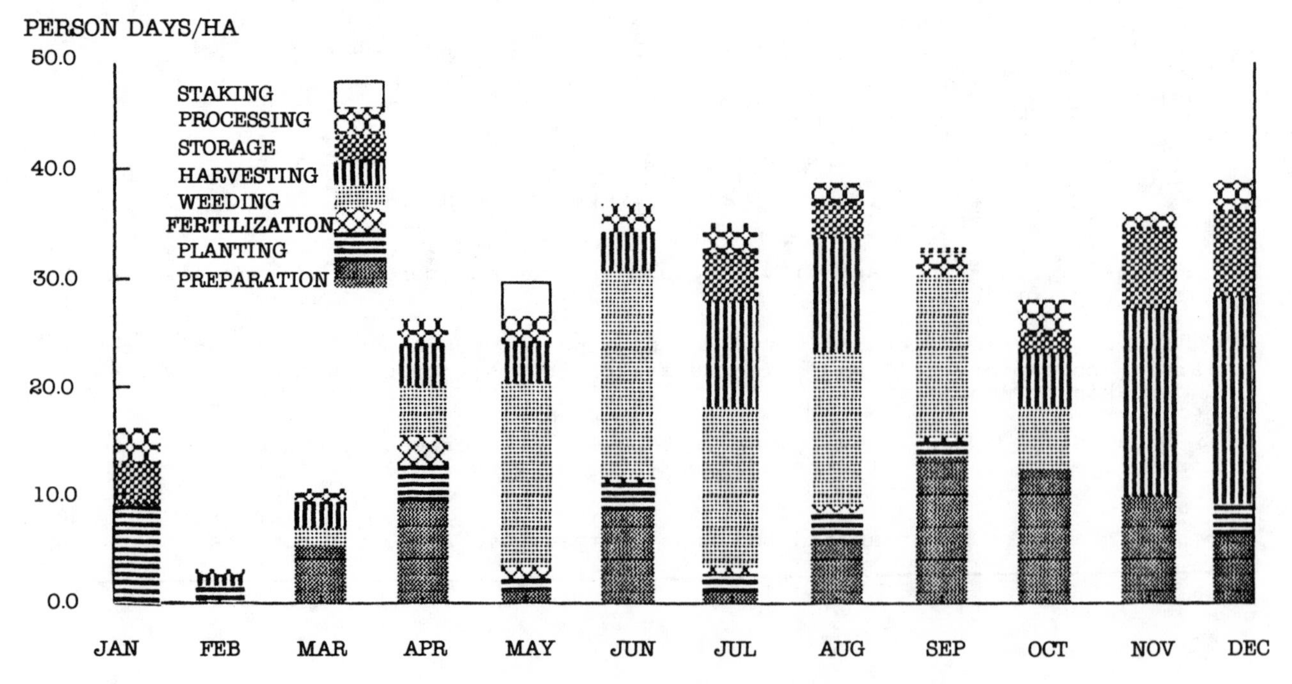

SOURCES: Bohannan and Bohannan, Tiv Economy; Vermeer, Agricultural and Dietary Practices Among the Tiv, Ibo and Birom Tribes, Nigeria; and Project Documents

CHART 3
FEMALE LABOR PROFILE (PRE-PROJECT)

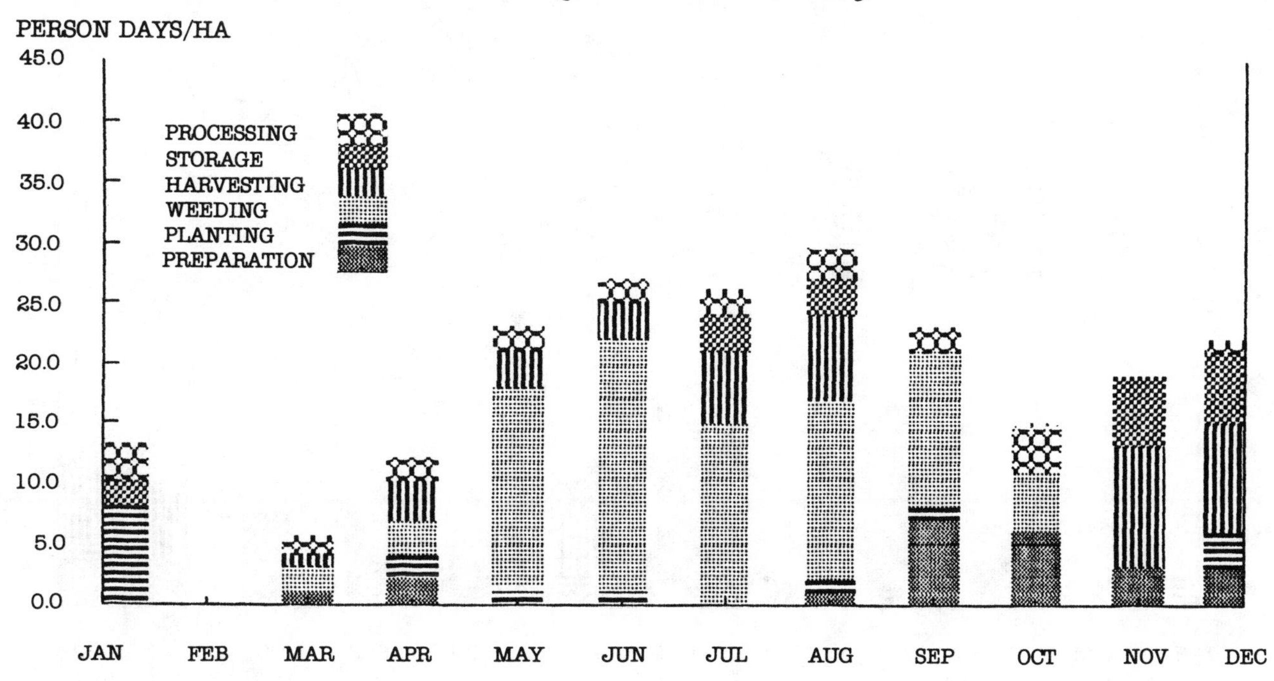

CHART 4
FEMALE LABOR PROFILE (POST-PROJECT)

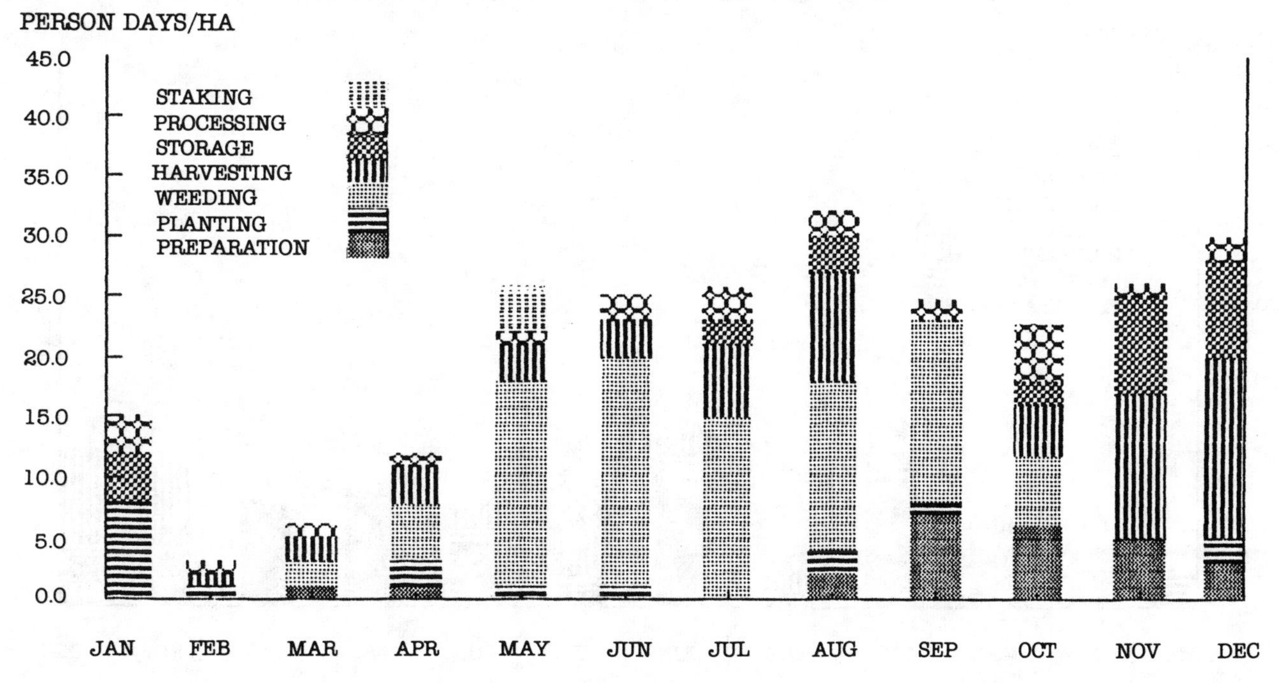

SOURCES: Bohannan and Bohannan, Tiv Economy; Vermeer, Agricultural and Dietary Practices Among the Tiv, Ibo and Birom Tribes, Nigeria; and Project Documents

CHART 5
MALE LABOR PROFILE (PRE-PROJECT)

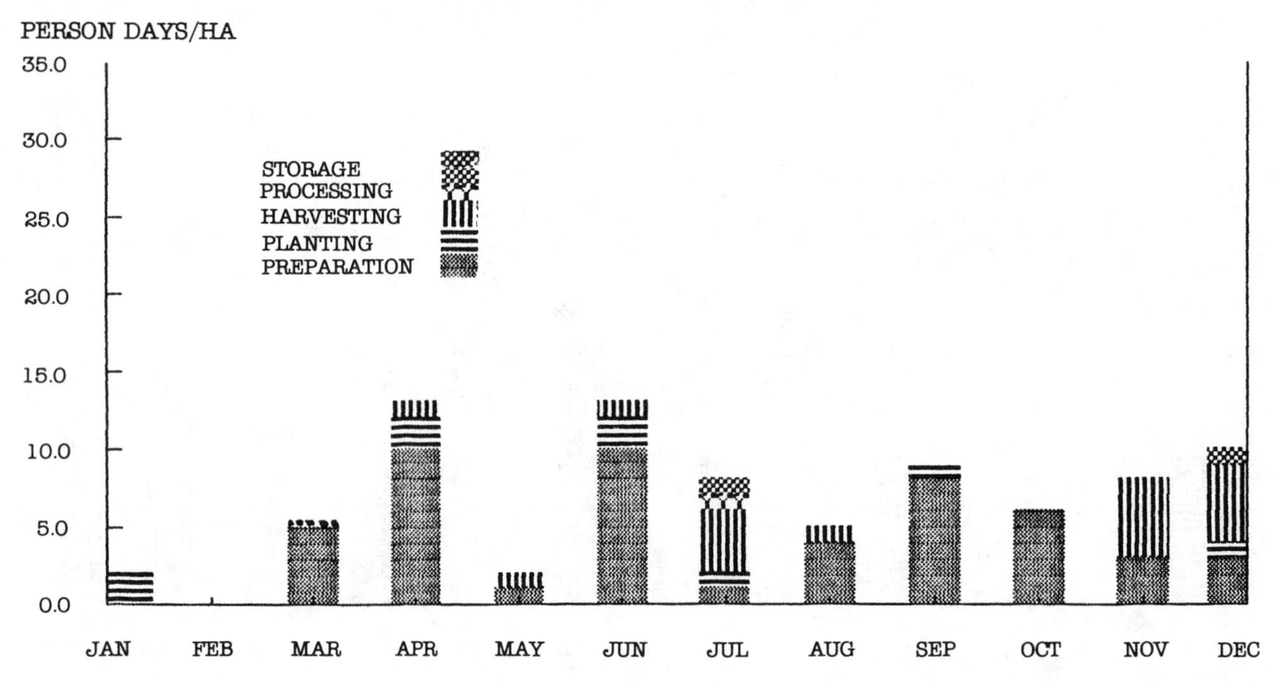

CHART 6
MALE LABOR PROFILE (POST-PROJECT)

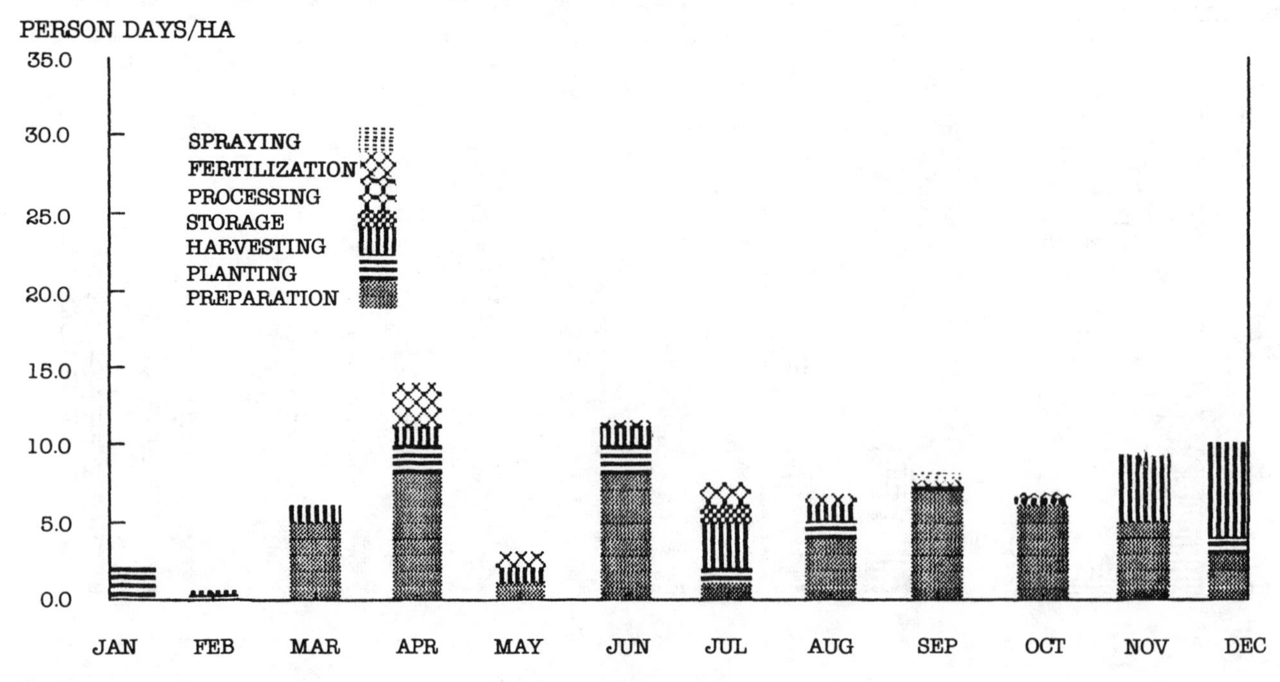

SOURCES: Bohannan and Bohannan, Tiv Economy; Vermeer, Agricultural and Dietary Practices Among the Tiv, Ibo and Birom Tribes, Nigeria; and Project Documents

Prior to the project, men's peak months of April, June, September and December differed from the peak months of the total farm (see Chart 5). The project has a more evenly distributed impact on men's seasonal labor requirements than it has on women's. Men's greatest labor increases occur in their non-peak months of May, August, and November, and represent slightly increased requirements for field preparation and new labor requirements for fertilizing and spraying. The project changes men's peak labor months only slightly, to April, June, November, and December (see Chart 6).

The greatest conflicts for Tiv women are likely to appear in May, June, and October. In all three of these months, about one-third of women's labor is allocated to crops for which men control all, or part, of the income. Specifically, in May and June, women's labor on men's millet, rice and melon crops competes with planting and weeding their own yam, maize, and sorghum crops. In October, women's labor on men's millet, rice, and melon competes with various tasks associated with their yam, cassava, and maize crops.

For Tiv men in the project area, conflicts are greatest in April, June, November, and December. In April and June, men's labor input on women's maize and sorghum crops conflicts with preparation and planting of melons, rice and millet and, in June, with millet harvest. Their arduous work in preparing yam mounds and yam planting in November and December conflicts with their rice harvest and with benniseed production. Men are furthermore likely to have less incentive than women to adopt spraying and fertilizing practices for yam, maize, and cowpeas, which are women's crops.

CHANGES IN INCOME

The second major objective of the project is to improve farm incomes. In the absence of data on actual farm incomes and expenditures, potential monetary benefit to farmers is estimated by the project from single crop budgets that calculate net returns per hectare and per person day. (See Table 3.) These calculations are made using projected farm-gate prices for inputs and outputs based on estimated yields under traditional or improved cultivation. The net return is thus the value of the total crop at projected market prices not the cost of seeds, fertilizers and insecticides. The change in net return per person day can be defined as the change in average productivity because it measures changes in output (returns) due to changes in input (labor). Specifically, it divides the net return, which is the value of total production, by the number of days worked, and measures the percent change in these values from before and after the project.

TABLE III: AREA, YIELDS AND RETURNS ON THE POST-PROJECT FARM [1]

CROP	Total area under cluti-vation [2]	Area under improved cultiva-tion	Change in yields under improved practices	Change in total net returns of crop
	HECTARES		PERCENT	
Yams	.625	.333	125	65
Cassava	.375	.083	150	11
Rice	.125	.050	125	8
Early Maize	.500	.333	133	45
Melon	.062	.029	100	43
Sorghum	.688	.200	100	15
Late Maize	.125	.075	192	107
Cowpeas	.125	.075	500	650
Benniseed	.188	.092	160	77

1 Based on post-project cropping pattern for typical 2.5 hectare farm.

2 Includes traditional, improved and advanced cultivation methods.

In this analysis, changes in labor requirements and net returns per person day are differentiated for women and men in the farm household. In Table 4 these are compared with changes anticipated on the basis of a corporate household. Data on changed labor requirements is broken down by crop. (See Appendix IV for labor profiles of the total farm, women and men, based on labor input by crop.) Data on changes in net returns per person day takes the labor impact of the project one step further; it looks at incentives by linking changes in labor with changes in income.

As discussed earlier, the measurement of income is based on the concept of control over returns, that is, control over the disposition of, and income from, a crop in order to meet obligations.

The linkage of control and meeting one's financial obligations means that a calculation of each sex's net returns, based on the proportion of the crop they control, reflects not only the opportunity to earn income but also the necessity to use that production, or returns, to meet specific obligations. This is a particularly important consideration in the context of subsistence farming and where local markets are not well developed. In this context, obligations toward family support are more strongly linked with production of particular crops.

In considering changes in net returns per person day across all crops, the differences between the total farm, women and men are not great. Women's returns per day of labor are increased by 31 percent, which is the same percentage increase anticipated for the total farm. Men's returns per day of labor are increased by 28 percent.

The reason women fare marginally better than men in this regard is because of their central role in controlling food crops (see Table 1), and the fact that these crops comprise most of the production increased by the project. Thus, women control more of the increase in production, or returns, from the project than men. This causes their daily net return to increase more than men's, who provide more labor on some home-consumed crops like maize and cowpeas but, because the crops are controlled by women, men do not get increased returns from their increased labor.

At the same time, it is important to note that the actual cash income component of net returns will most likely be much smaller than the in-kind (actual crop) component. This will vary with the crop, but may be particularly true for women's crops, since women's major responsibilities involve production of food crops for family consumption. But this depends on what women consider surplus for sale, as well as on market opportunities. Men's net returns, however, may have a larger cash income component due to their greater responsibilities for crops which are marketed.

These indicators of total change also miss some significant differences in returns on individual crops. Data in Table 4 illustrate the relative differences in incentives on each crop between the aggregate and disaggregated farm and also between women and men. Particularly pronounced is the lack of incentives for men to contribute to crops used by women to feed the family, and the differences in incentives to increase labor on benniseed

TABLE IV: CHANGES IN THE LABOR AND NET RETURNS BY CROP FOR THE TOTAL FARM, WOMEN AND MEN[1]

CROP	TOTAL FARM	
	Change in labor input[2]	Change in net returns[2]
Yams	24	33
Cassava	-1	11
Rice	-21	37
Early Maize	5	38
Millet	-3.1	0
Melon	24	15
Sorghum	4	11
Late Maize	43	44
Cowpeas	257	108
Benniseed	37	29

	WOMEN		MEN	
	Change in labor input	Change in net returns[2]	Change in labor input	Changes in net returns[2]
Yams	25	33	17	43
Cassava	-1	12	2	9
Rice	-20	33	-23	40
Early Maize	4	9	0	
Millet	-12	0	-13	0
Melon	27	13	18	21
Sorghum	2	13	6	0
Late Maize	43	45	44	0
Cowpeas	238	122	280	0
Benniseed	61	9	10	61

1 Net return measures the value of total production at market prices projected by the project, net of costs of inputs, based on the cropping patterns of a 2.5 ha hypothetical farm.

2 Change in net return per person/day is calculated as $\frac{Y_2 - Y_1}{L - L_1}$ $\frac{Y_1}{L_1}$

where y_1 is net return pre-project, y is net return post-project, L_1 is number of person/days of labor pre-project and L_2 is number of person days of labor post-project. For income date, (Y) see Table 1 and Appendix 5. For data on the labor requirements of women, men, and the total farm, by crop, see Appendix VI.

Sources: Bohannan, Vermeer, and Project Documents.

and melon, which are marketed crops from which men derive their income.

The juxtaposition of the change in labor requirements with the changes in net daily returns, as presented in Table 4, is also an important factor to consider because labor availability is a critical constraint to production in this area. Comparing the two figures illustrates the magnitude of the labor increase that is required to achieve the anticipated increases in returns, a magnitude that one sex may find difficult to absorb. A comparison of the changes in annual labor input for each crop for the total farm, and for women and men, in order to achieve the expected increase in returns indicates substantial differences for benniseed, yams, early maize and melons. As discussed above, however, changes in the seasonality of labor are as critical to consider as changes in total labor.

IMPLICATIONS

The introduction of new technologies inevitably changes labor requirements for most crops and tasks. By increasing the volume of production, these interventions also increase the returns from crops. However, the existence of sex-differentiated labor roles, income sources, and financial responsibilities results in different impacts of project interventions on women and men. These differential impacts have implications for project design and for the achievement of project objectives.

One implication of the role differences in the Tiv farm household is that the introduction and adoption of new technologies and other innovations cannot depend upon pooled farm family labor as a resource or on shared family income as an incentive. Our analysis demonstrates how the labor requirements and financial incentives of the project can differ for each sex because of their different roles.

A second implication is that different roles can create conflicts in labor allocations between men and women which can have a negative impact on the achievement of project objectives. For Tiv women in the project area, conflicts in labor allocation are likely to be most critical during peak farming months, when demands on their time from all farming activities are greatest. Conflicts may also occur in months where the project has created significant new demands for their labor but where a high proportion of this labor is used on male controlled crops. Women's sources of income and financial responsibilities are likely to be an important determinant of how these conflicts are resolved. Of course, the within-household exchange between women and men, already described, may over time be developed and expanded further to facilitate the diffusion of incentives to the partner who shares in the additional labor requirement.

A third implication of differing roles in the Tiv farm household relates to the fact that technologies increase the productivity of some tasks and not others. Overall, women's labor requirements on crops targeted by the project were increased more than men's because many of the tasks for which women have sole or primary responsibility, such as harvesting and processing, were not improved by the project. Disproportionate labor increases for one sex may mean that sex is simply unable to absorb the magnitude of the new labor requirements of the project. The absence of improvements on certain crops or tasks can also result in differences in each sex's productivity within the household, in terms of returns per day of labor.

Related to this is the fact that many farm household activities are not addressed by the project. In addition to production of major crops, there are a number of "non-project" activities such as gathering fuel wood and water, food preparation, and child care which are also critical to the survival of the household.

While project documents provide little information on the time spent by family members on activities other than the project crops, these requirements and obligations are likely to be considerable. For women in particular, some of these commitments such as cooking, gathering of fuel wood, water hauling and child care, may not be flexible enough to permit a greater allocation of time to the project's crops. Fuel wood, for instance, is in short supply in the Tiv area according to project documents. In a more densely populated location about 180km. southwest of the project area, fuel and water collection consumes one to three hours daily. Preparation of the foods the Tiv eat requires one to two hours per meal with one to three meals prepared daily.[10] In addition, the greatest additional labor demands created by the project for Tiv women, in October through November, coincide with the harvesting and storage requirements for women's side crops, which are not considered or improved by the project. These crops are used for sauces and represent an important nutritional component of the diet.

If there are conflicts between non-project activities and the additional labor demands of project activities, adoption of project interventions may be reduced. It is consequently important to consider labor input on non-project activities, particularly during the peak labor periods. `In this context, the links between project and non-project activities, between labor expended and income earned, and the contribution of certain tasks to the fulfillment of various obligations need to be carefully examined.

Linking changes in labor and changes in income for each sex can also highlight areas in which a potential exists for reduced incentives of one sex to adopt more labor-intensive technologies for the other's crop. For example, Tiv men are expected to increase their labor on cowpeas by 280 percent, but they derive no income from this crop. Women are expected to increase their labor input on benniseed, a male cash crop, by 61 percent although their financial incentive is limited (see Table 4).

Incentives play a crucial role in determining if, and to what extent, new technologies are adopted by members of the farming household. The "diversion of incentives" can undermine a project.[11] The lack of incentive to contribute, or to increase labor inputs, particularly when this labor would compete with one's own income-generating activities, can result in the withdrawal of one sex's labor input or refusal to adopt new technologies or innovations. This in turn can be a constraint on raising agricultural production and raising standards of living in rural areas. On the other hand, incentives can create shifts in labor role, at times resulting in the economic marginalization of one sex. Studies have documented for example how men may shift into a woman's crop that has become more lucrative. Among the Tiv, rice was a woman's crop until its market value increased in the early 1970s. Now men dominate its cultivation and earnings.

Finally, non-financial incentives can also be important in providing a context within which to judge women's and men's contribution to a particular task and their use of time. Since women have primary responsibility for providing food for the family, they may place priority on subsistence food crop production despite the significant labor requirements.

The value of leisure time and the relative status of household members in terms of their labor, productivity and income are among the non-financial incentives that may also be important to consider in the project context.

CONCLUSIONS

ALTERNATIVE DESIGNS FOR THE PROJECT

There are several general and specific project design changes that could alleviate the effect of, or at least take into account, the within-household divisions of the Tiv, and contribute to the achievement of the project objectives.

The most general change that should be made is the incorporation of an explicit recognition of the central role of Tiv women in many of the project's crops and of the differences in female and male labor roles, income sources and financial responsibilities. In particular, the almost total absence of references to the different needs and incentives of women farmers in the project area implies that the project is unlikely to ensure their participation or their receipt of project benefits, apart from their membership in the amorphous total farm. Experience indicates that when women are not explicitly considered in project plans, there is usually an underlying assumption that their interests are incorporated in male farmers' interests, [12] and it is unlikely that women will be given explicit recognition in later project stages. [13]

The most pressing need is for the project to address the inequitable distribution of increased labor requirements between women and men, and the potential for women not to adopt technologies due to their inability to absorb labor increases of this magnitude, particularly in their processing and storage activities. Rather than decrease the volume of production, the project could focus on increasing efficiency and productivity in women's tasks.

According to project documents, there are provisional plans to establish an itinerant home economics team, but not until the fifth year of the project. The delay in starting this program and its provisional nature is an indication that the project is not emphasizing some important farm household needs, particularly those farm activities not undertaken by men. More importantly, the lack of home economics program exacerbates the problem of Tiv women absorbing much of the increased labor requirements due to the project. Without a home economics component, without food processing or food storage innovations, Tiv women in the project area will be expected to handle far greater volumes of farm production with no improvements in these tasks' productivity. The burden represented by the heavy labor increases associated with these tasks could be a major disincentive for women to adopt project technologies on both their own and on men's crops. Clearly the Tiv division of labor will necessitate project activities to improve the farm's ability to handle the anticipated increase in the volume of crop production.

Improving processing and storage techniques could provide several advantages in addition to improving women's capacity to handle the increased production. To the extent that processing and storage of non-project crops may create a bottleneck for women in November and December, improving their efficiency in these tasks could ease an important constraint to their adoption of project technologies. In addition, developing food processing technologies could develop, or improve, the potential for the sale of processed food as a source of cash income for women farmers.

There is also a need for the project to underscore the outreach of extension services to women farmers. This is a very typical area in which projects fail to serve women. 14

Project interventions are more likely to be adopted by both female and male farmers if the primary agent of change, the extension service, is targeted toward them both. The primary means of communication in this project is a mobile audio-visual module. Recognizing women's central role in the production of many of the project crops, particularly in yams, and the lack of incentive for men to innovate in some of their crops, these services need to be targeted explicitly to reach both women and men, to provide information relevant to their complementary work on crops, and particularly to reach the appropriate sex with the project information most relevant to them.

In the project's fourth year, one-week residential training will be offered to farmers at project headquarters. Residential training presents logistical problems for women, who also have responsibilities for child care and daily housekeeping and cooking tasks. If these in-depth training courses are not to exclude female farmers, explicit attention must be given to identifying and resolving conflicts that may prevent women's attendance. For example, visiting extension workers could be briefed to counterbalance this effective discrimination.

The project's well building, forestry and road building activities have the potential both for improving the infrastructure needed to support crop development, and for saving time for women in non-project activities such as water-hauling and fuel collection. The project documents do not explicitly recognize the implications of reducing women's labor on non-project activities for the ability of women to adopt project technologies. However, this is an important point to raise because it will help the project to better define priorities and design for these support activities.

While the project can exert little control over the local and national farm context, its ability to achieve its objectives will be enhanced if it takes these factors into account because they may exacerbate differential impacts of the project on women and men in the farm household.

The price and marketing conditions in the project area may cause differential access to income from marketed crops. For example, Tiv women and men earn their income from different crops; improvement of marketing channels should thus take into account the need to provide both sexes' crops with market development assistance. To the extent that marketing in the project area becomes more organized, perhaps through a reorganization of the presently weak cooperative, the dominant role of Tiv women in market trading should be explicitly recognized and women should be encouraged to participate in market development. Finally, the project causes yams, a women's crop, to have the greatest absolute increases in value of production. Women's control over this important source of food and income should be recognized and supported or yams will become a male crop, as rice did in the 1950s.

The local political structure, which is used by the project as a communication channel with local people, does not provide equal representation for women and men. Only men may be elected to the council of elders. Because men's and women's interests and responsibilities differ, however, the project should ensure that women have direct access to project personnel and do not have to rely on men for communication of their interests. This might be done by including any existing women's organizations on the local project committee.

The Tiv land tenure system, in which women depend on their husbands for access to land, can potentially erode women's access to land, their ability to earn a living and the local production of women's food crops. According to project documents, population growth and migration to the area are increasing population density and land pressure. Improved agricultural productivity might also contribute to increasing land values. Rising land values and increased crop commercialization have in some areas led to a diversion of land toward greater production of marketed crops or toward men's sale or lease of their land without allocating sufficient land to their wives. Women thus lose access to fields and livelihood, and their families' nutrition may suffer. Women's control over land and their participation in household decision-making can be safeguarded or improved by ensuring that their productivity and income are improved equally with men's by project activities.

Education in the project area can affect project results through its effects on child labor availability and because of the need for non-formal adult literacy and numeracy training. Nigeria's passage of the Universal Primary Education Act is likely to increasingly draw child labor off the farms where they assist in planting and scaring birds. Tiv children also have major child care responsibilities, which are likely to revert to adult women. These added responsibilities on Tiv women make project efforts to improve women's productivity in project and household activities even more imperative.

The project area is located in an educationally disadvantaged state and it is likely that both women and men adults have a high rate of illiteracy. Educational efforts through the extension program and other projects should attempt to reach both sexes with the necessary training and education for their different farm and household roles.

Farm credit in the project area is also not as likely to have important differential implications because of its limited availability for both sexes. However, women's lack of direct land holding rights and their lack of direct political access can potentially weaken their credit worthiness, if credit becomes an option in the future. Therefore the project should strengthen women's informal credit institutions.

In general, it will be important for the project to periodically assess and monitor the extent to which improved practices are being adopted and how these practices are distributed between crops. This distribution will influence changes in annual and seasonal workloads by sex, and likely personal income returns. The project's estimates of the proportion of a crop cultivated by improved means is speculative. Because of the linkage between labor and incentives, there is a case for establishing a farm systems component that would provide farmers and project management with a two-way exchange on the most profitable division of traditional and improved methods for each crop. Similarly, women's and men's access to extension and credit services needs to be monitored.

SUMMARY AND CONCLUSIONS

It is in the context of the current food and agricultural situation in Sub-Saharan Africa that more detailed farm level analysis is so urgently needed. Problems of stagnant or declining agricultural productivity in many countries of the region cannot be dealt with at the macro level only. Agricultural development projects can provide a more localized focus for a country's development effort. But if these projects are meant to be a positive force of change in the lives of rural people, then planners will need to better understand the structure and dynamics of the environment in which they are operating. A critical aspect of this understanding is the sharply differentiated roles and responsibilities of women and men which alter the resources and constraints of the total farm and which affect the ability and incentives of each sex to adopt project technologies.

In our analysis we test and accept the hypotheses that the amount and seasonality of female and male labor requirements, as well as their income levels and income earning opportunities, will be affected differently by project interventions because of their different roles and responsibilities in the farm household.

This suggests that the intended impact, anticipated on the basis of total farm resources, is different enough from that anticipated on a disaggregated basis to warrant within-household analyses of farm operations at the project planning stage.

Agricultural development planners are often confronted with an inadequate data base concerning those people they wish to target--subsistence farmers. Much of the inadequacy stems from definitional problems at the national level: the conventional definition of labor force tends to cover only those who are wage earners. Data concerning women suffer from even greater limitations because of the statistically arbitrary line between economic and non-economic activities. The latter category encompasses activities for which there may be no direct financial remuneration, such as processing and preparing food for the family, or childcare, but which are crucial to the livelihood of the household and represent important resources of the total farm household. There are also inadequacies concerning the specificity of data: geographical and ethnic variations need to be taken into account.

At the project design stage there is a need for sex-disaggregated socio-economic baseline data. This will facilitate the analysis of work patterns, labor requirements and financial interactions and obligations within the farming household. If the household is viewed as an integrated production and consumption unit, then all relevant activities can be included, without making the generally misleading distinction between farm and non-farm activities. This categorization tends to obscure women's predominant role in activities which are not strictly related to crop production and to bypass activities that may have an effect on the farm household's response to project interventions.

Midterm evaluations of projected impacts on members of the farming household will be all the more effective if comprehensive baseline data are available. If this is not the case, the evaluation can point out weaknesses in project design that may be related to sex role differences and suggest ways in which subsequent phases of the project can better target individuals within farm households.

From a methodological perspective, a farming systems approach that incorporates all of the household's production and consumption activities, rather than only crops improved by the project, can be useful in addressing weaknesses in planning since it provides a framework for analyzing the linkages between individual farm households and their environment. It is crucial, however, to use this approach to go beyond the household as a unit of analysis and to assess the intra-household divisions of labor and income.

Distinguishing between women's and men's roles and considering the implications of these role differences is crucial to the process of improving productivity and income. Too long perceived as a social welfare issue, the concept of women's role in development needs to be perceived for what it is: an important productivity issue that should be a standard part of the planning process. If one goal of development is ultimately the integration of both women and men, then the different needs and incentives of each must be explicitly recognized and addressed so that projects and program can become responsive to the people they are designed to assist.

ENDNOTES

1 See John C. DeWilde, *Experiences with Agricultural Development in Tropical Africa*, Two volumes, (Baltimore: John Hopkins Press, 1967); John C. Cleave, *African Farmers: Labor Use in the Development of Smallholder Agriculture* (New York: Praeger, 1974); D.W. Norman, David Pryor, and Christopher Gibbs, *Technical Change and the Small Farmer in Hausaland, Northern Nigeria* African Rural Economy Paper, No. 21, (Michigan State University, 1979); Cheryl Christensen et al, *Food Problems and Prospects in Sub-Saharan Africa: The Decade of the 1980's*, U.S. Department of Agriculture, FAER No. 166, 1981.

2 See for example Ester Boserup, *Women's Role in Economic Development* (New York: St. Martin's Press, 1970) and Nancy Hafkin and Edna Bay, eds., *Women in Africa: Studies in Social and Economic Change* (Stanford: Stanford University Press, 1976).

3 United Nations Economic Commission for Africa, Human Resources Division, "Women: The Neglected Human Resource for African Development," in *Canadian Journal of African Studies*, Vol. 6, No. 2, 1972. See also Brenda McSweeney, "Collection and Analysis of Data on Rural Women's Time Use," in Sondra Zeidenstein, ed., *Studies in Family Planning: Learning About Rural Women* (Nov./Dec. 1979).

4 Kathleen Cloud, *Sex Roles in Food Production and Food Distribution System in the Sahel*, Agency for International Development, December 15, 1977.

5 Ruth Dixon, *Assessing the Impact of Development Projects on Women*, AID Program Evaluation Discussion Paper No. 8, Office of Women in Development and Office of Evaluation, U.S. Agency for International Development, Washington, D.C., 1980.

6 Ingrid Palmer, *The Nemow Case*, The Population Council, 1979.

7 See A. U. Patel and Q. B. Anthonio, "Farmers' Wives in Agricultural Development: The Nigerian Case," University of Ibadan, Nigeria, (paper prepared for the 15th International Congress of Agricultural Economics, Sao Paulo, Brazil, August 1973); and Tomilayo Adeyokunna, "Women and Agriculture in Nigeria," Department of Agricultural Economics, University of Ibadan, Ibadan, Nigeria, February 1980.

8 See Polly Hill, "Hidden Trade in Hausaland," *Man*. Vol. 4, No. 3, September 1969; and Simmons, 1975 (check with author).

9 Richard Longhurst, *Rural Development Planning and the Sexual Division of Labor: A Case Study of a Moslem Hausa Village in Northern Nigeria*, Geneva: ILO, 1980.

10 Celia Jean Weidemann, "Case Studies of Five Rural Families in Eastern Nigeria: Implications for Planning Home Economics Extension Programmes," *Home Economics Research Bulletin*, No. 1, May 1977.

11 See for example Raymond Apthorpe, "Some Problems of Evaluation," in Carl Wistrand, ed., *Cooperatives and Rural Development in East Africa*, (New York: Africans Publishing Corporation, 1970).

12 Barbara Rogers, *The Domestication of Women* (New York: St. Martin's Press, 1979)

13 Ruth Dixon, *Assessing the Impact of Development Projects on Women*, AID Program Evaluation Discussion Paper No. 8, Office of Women in Development and Office of Evaluation, U.S. Agency for International Development, Washngton, D.C., 1980.

14 See for example Kathleen Staudt, "Development Interventions and Differential Technology Impact Between Men and Women,' (paper presented at the Third World Conference, University of Nebraska at Omaha, October 24-27, 1979).

APPENDIXES

APPENDIX I. LABOR REQUIREMENTS OF THE TEN CROPS ON TYPICAL FARM

The charts below give labor profiles by crop and crop activity under both traditional and improved farm practices. These tables are useful in that, for individual crops, they show the breakdown and timing of activities, and the differences in total labor requirements for each activity using different techniques. The improved cultivation practices include the use of high yielding varieties, fertilizers and pesticides. Under these methods, there are new tasks such as fertilizing and additional time requirements for other tasks due primarily to the increase in yields and production. These tables also compare the labor requirements of different crops. For example, to produce one hectare of yams (see Chart 1) requires many more person days than one hectare of melons (see Chart 10).

APPENDIX I

CHART 1 : YAMS

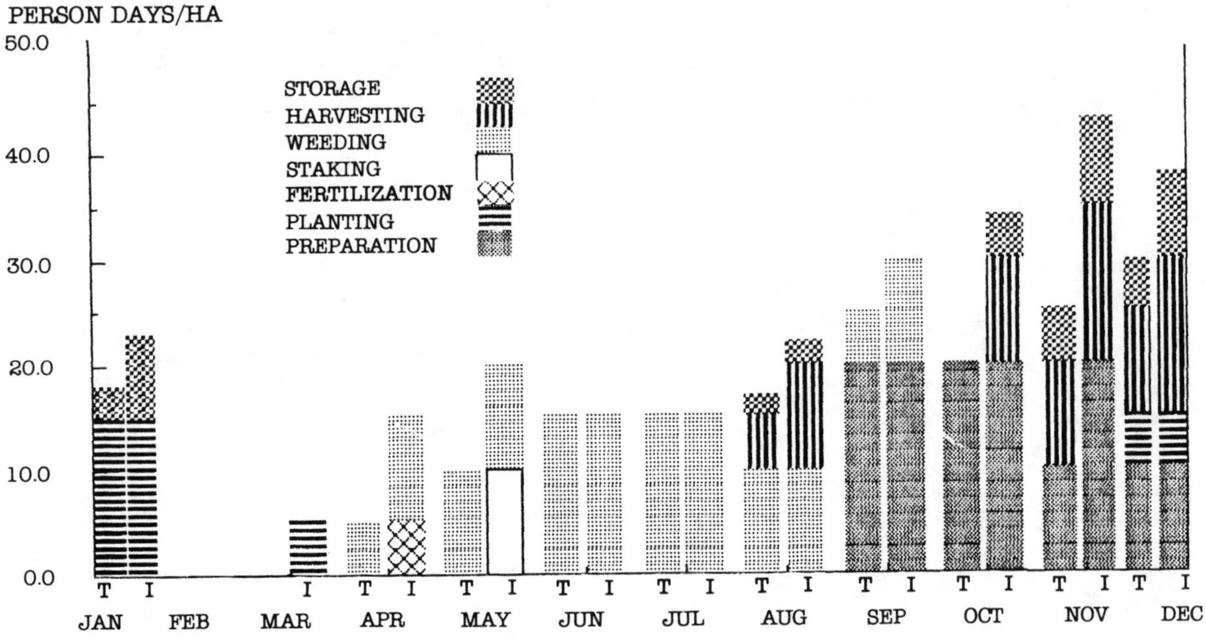

PERSON DAYS/HA

50.0
40.0
30.0
20.0
10.0
0.0

STORAGE
HARVESTING
WEEDING
STAKING
FERTILIZATION
PLANTING
PREPARATION

T I I T I T I T I T I T I T I T I T I T I
JAN FEB MAR APR MAY JUN JUL AUG SEP OCT NOV DEC

T=TRADITIONAL
I=IMPROVED

SOURCE: Project Documents

APPENDIX I

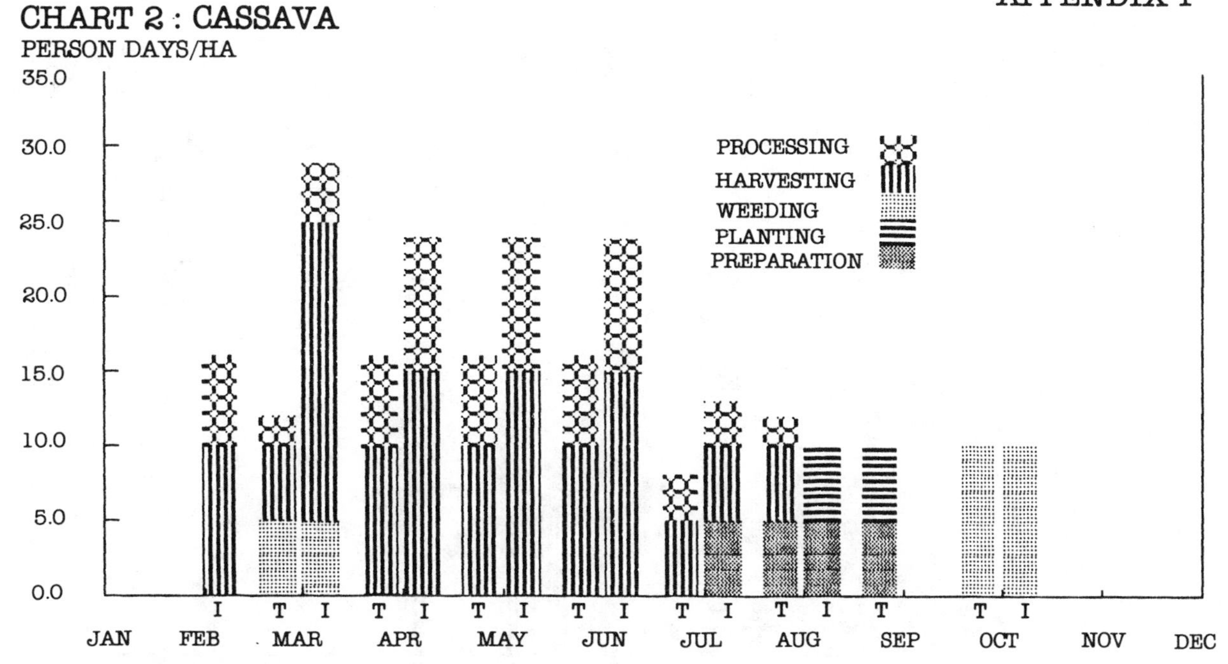

T=TRADITIONAL
I=IMPROVED

SOURCE: Project Documents

APPENDIX I

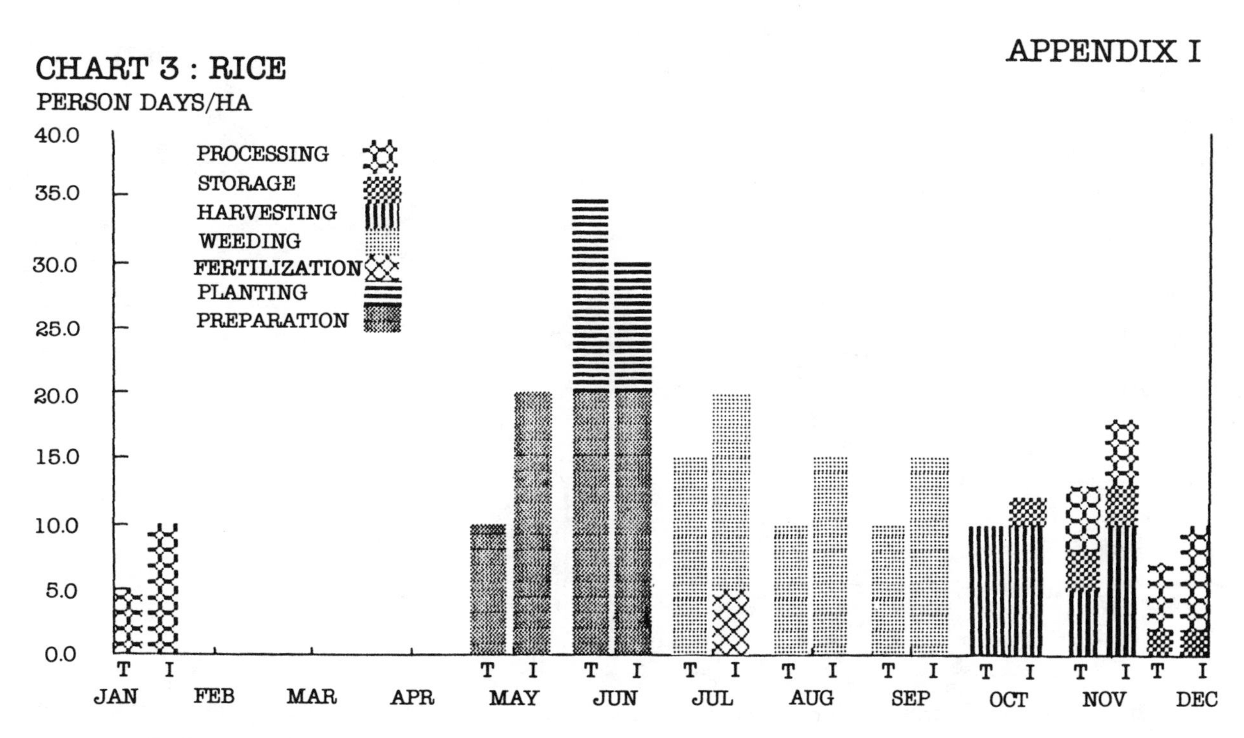

T=TRADITIONAL
I=IMPROVED

SOURCE: Project Documents

APPENDIX I

CHART 4 : EARLY MAIZE

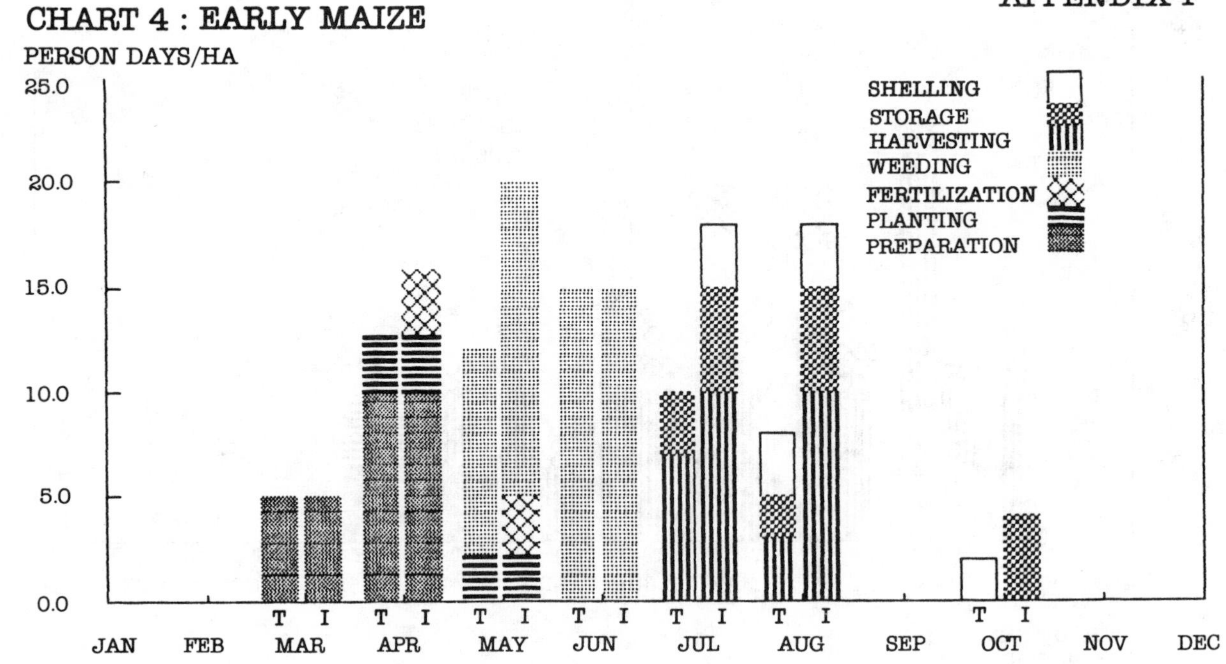

T=TRADITIONAL
I=IMPROVED

SOURCE: Project Documents

APPENDIX I

CHART 5 : EARLY MILLET

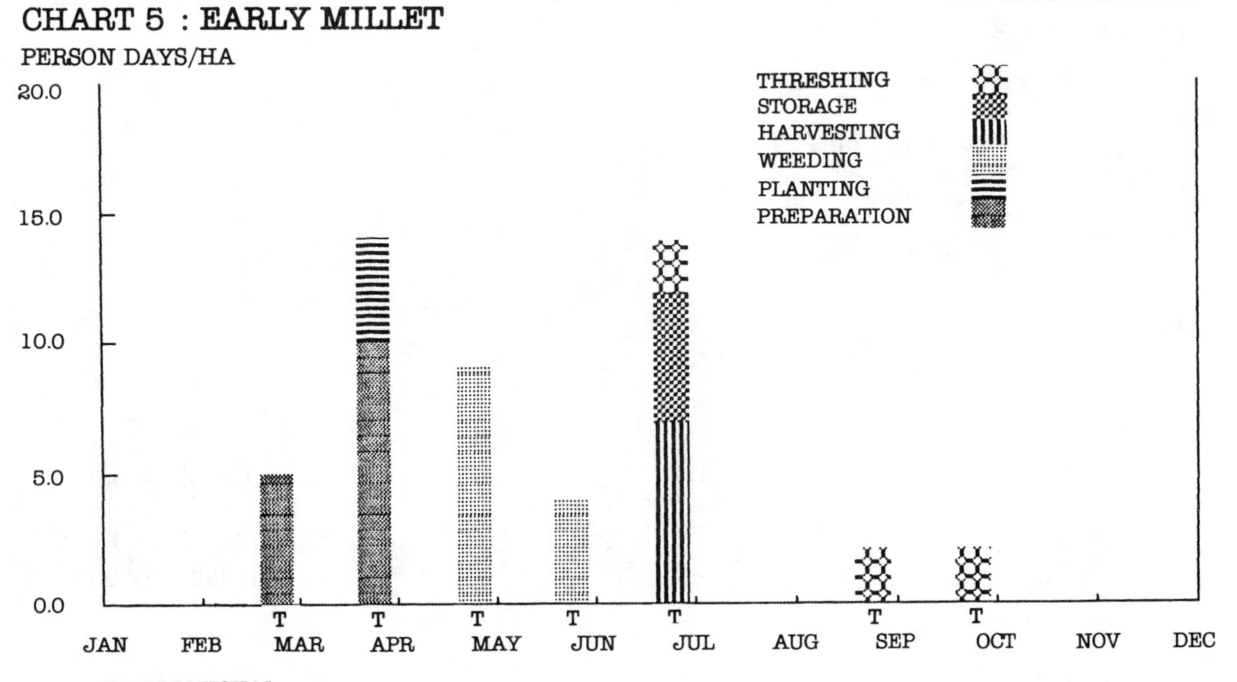

T=TRADITIONAL

SOURCE: Project Documents

CHART 6 : SORGHUM

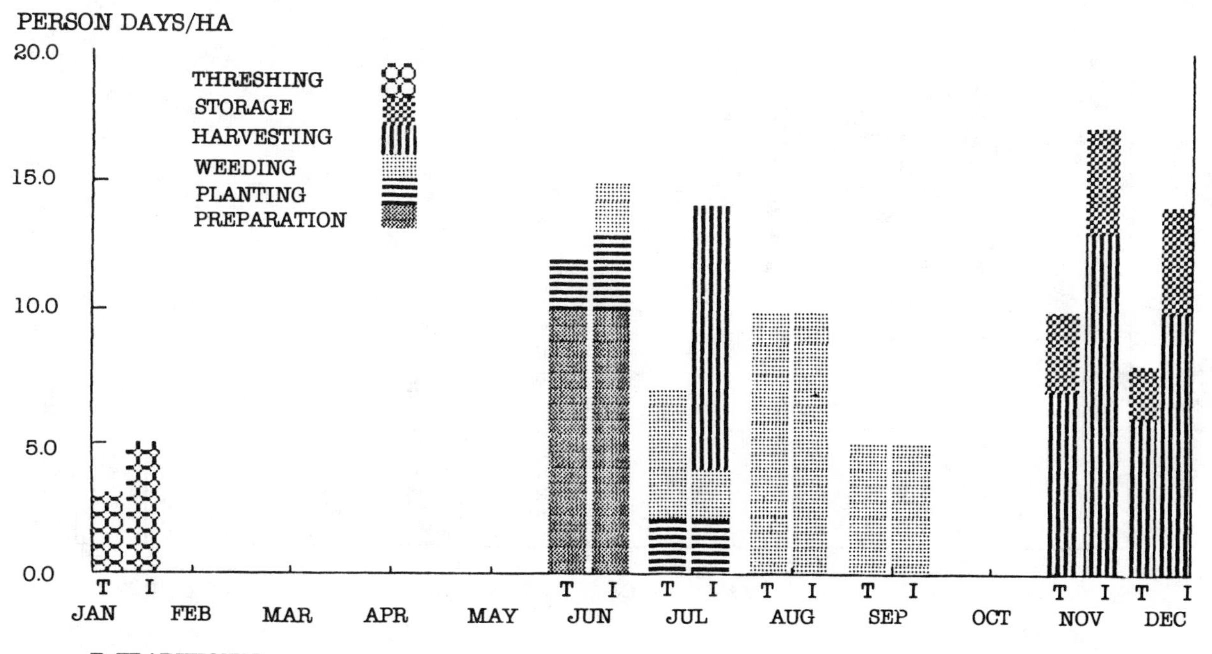

T=TRADITIONAL
I=IMPROVED

SOURCE: Project Documents

APPENDIX I

CHART 7 : LATE MAIZE

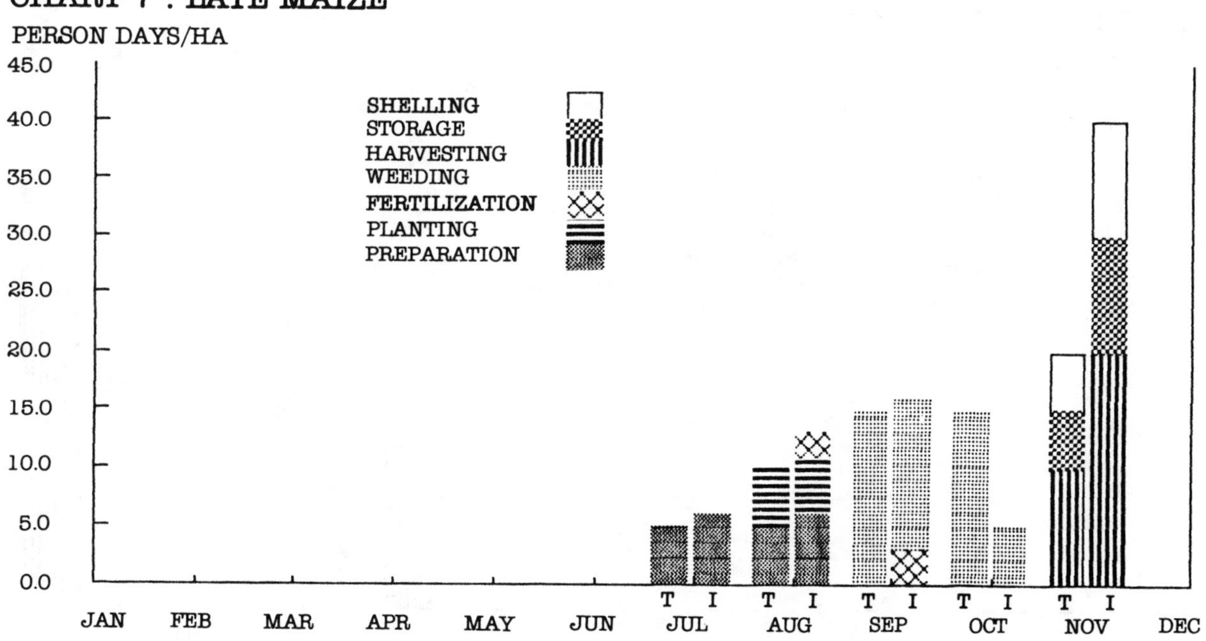

T=TRADITIONAL
I=IMPROVED

SOURCE: Project Documents

CHART 8 : COWPEAS

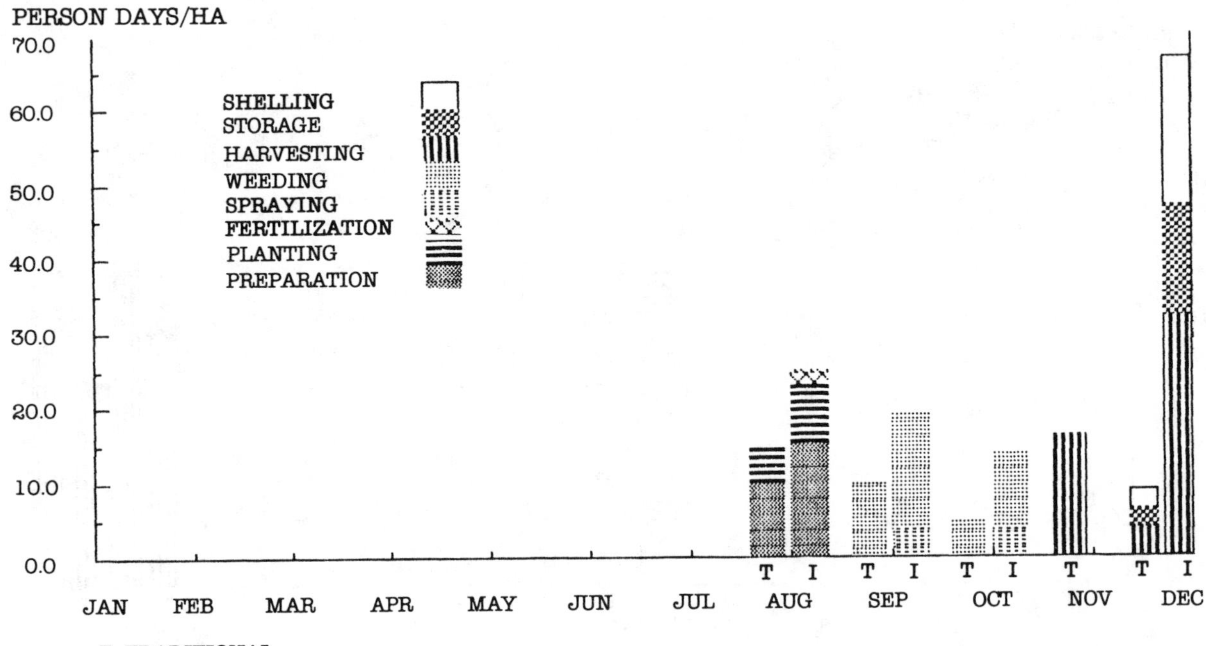

T=TRADITIONAL
I=IMPROVED

SOURCE: Project Documents

APPENDIX I

CHART 9 : BENNISEED

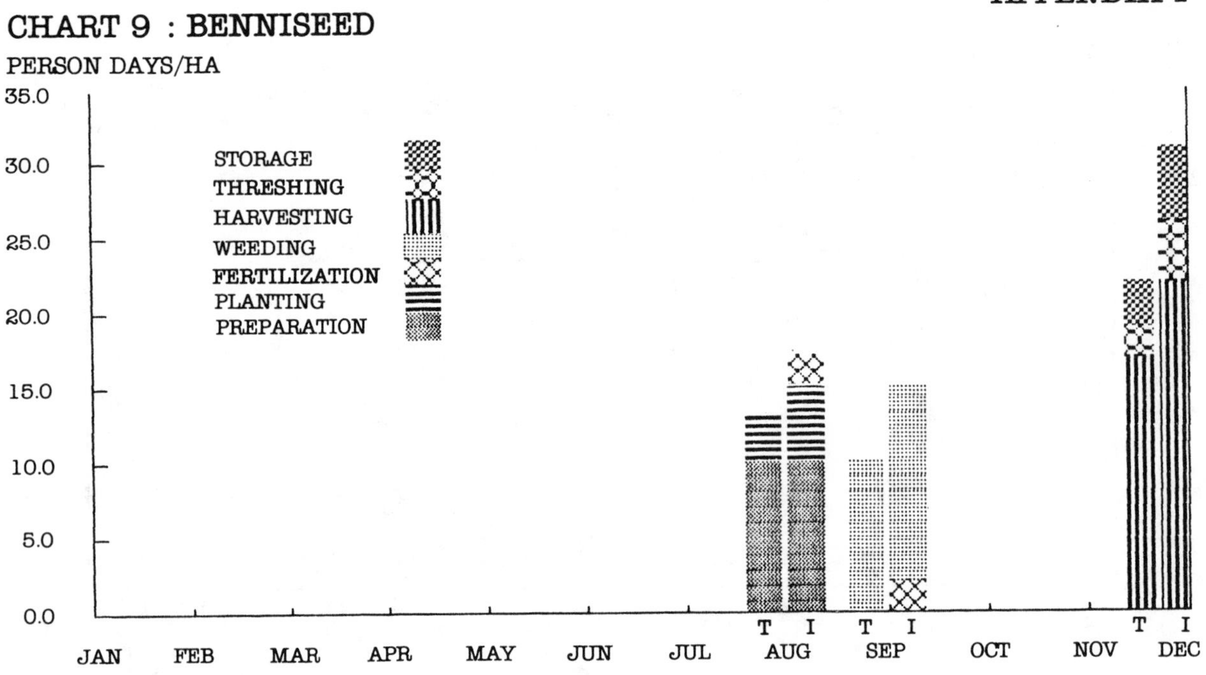

T=TRADITIONAL
I=IMPROVED

SOURCE: Project Documents

APPENDIX I

CHART 10 : MELON

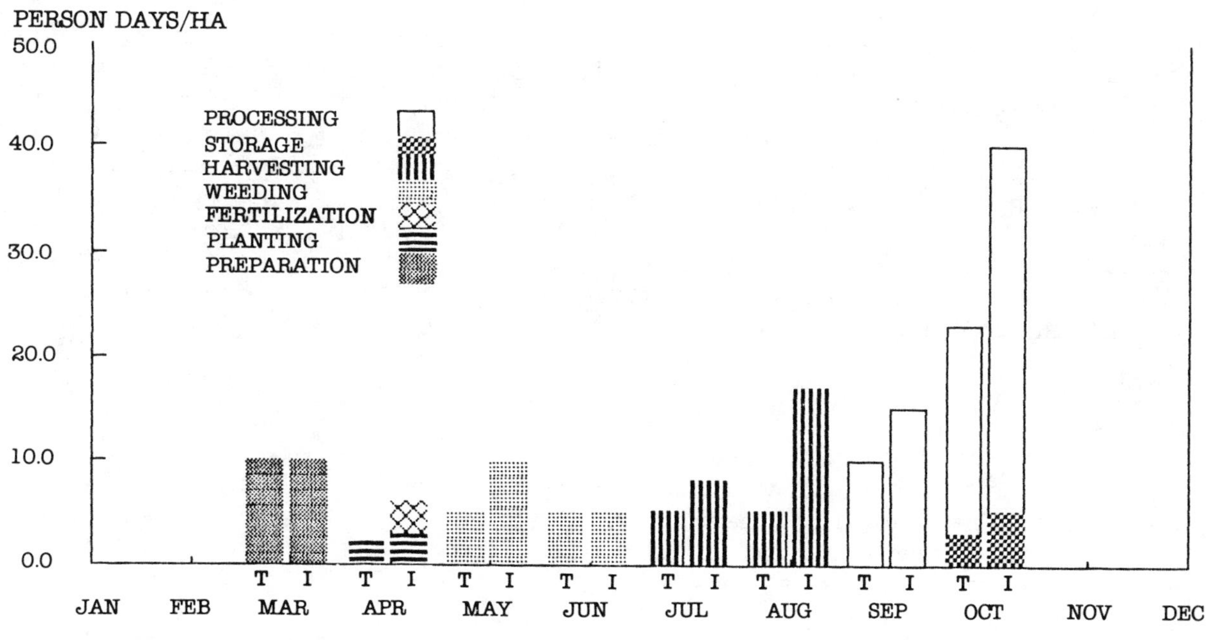

T=TRADITIONAL
I=IMPROVED

SOURCE: Project Documents

APPENDIX II. DIVISION OF LABOR IN THE PRODUCTION OF STAPLE CROPS

In Appendix II below, the contributions of male and female farmers to the production of crops being affected by the agricultural development project are discussed in detail. Tiv women have a greater labor input than men into yams, sorghum, cowpeas and maize, all of which are important subsistence crops in this region. Men have a relatively greater labor input into millet and melons. Both sexes contribute about equally to rice, cassava and benniseed, which are important as both food crop and as locally marketed crops.

Yams

Yam is the first crop grown in the bush/fallow cycle. One field for each woman is cleared from the bush at the beginning of the dry season in October and November. During the first few days of field clearing, the whole compound helps to pull up grasses.

Within a few days, the men shift to cutting down sapling and low branches of larger trees and later to building yam mounds. Women continue to pull up grasses and are also responsible for burning and killing large trees by ringing them with live cinders. As the mounds are built, women, their daughters and sometimes men, plant the seed yams. When the yams are planted, men's involvement with the crop is finished. Women are responsible for staking, weeding, harvesting, processing and storage.

Female/Male Labor Contribution to Yam Production

Crop	Field Prep.	Planting	Weeding	Harvesting	Processing	Storage
Yam	F: 50% M: 50%	F: 80% M: 20	F	F	F	F

The first weeding of the yam field is in March, shortly after the start of the rainy season. As the women work in the yam fields they plant a number of crops on the sides or at the bottom of the mounds. The number of side crops can be large and may include staple crops such as cassava or maize, and many varieties of vegetables. Intercropped plants on women's yam mounds provide many of the vegetables used in stews and sauces, which are an important nutritional component of the Tiv diet. Side crops also represent an important, independent source of what are otherwise male controlled crops grown on the men's fields. For instance, women who grow millet, a male crop, thus have their own source of that grain for brewing into beer for sale.

After harvest, yams are sorted and stored in airy, thatched shelters. Seed yams for the following year are stored in elevated platforms inside the compound. Yam is the most important food crop in this region and is prepared for eating in a variety of ways.

Millet

Millet, considered a male crop, is the second crop in the bush/fallow cycle, although some may be intercropped with the woman's yams. Men handle field preparation for millet which involves breaking down and leveling the old yam mounds. When the field is ready, men plant the seed, with some assistance from women, by broadcasting it and turning over the soil to bury it. Occasionally, it is planted by dropping the seeds into holes made in old mounds with the heel of the foot.

Female/Male Labor Contribution to Millet Production

Crop	Field Prep.	Planting	Weeding	Harvesting	Processing	Storage
Millet	M	F: 20% M: 80%	F	F: 50% M: 50%	F	F: 50% M: 50%

Women do all weeding for millet. Both men and women work on millet harvesting with men breaking down the stalks while women cut off and pile the heads of grain. Men tie the heads of millet into bundles which women carry back to the compound. Millet is sometimes stored in shacks on the bush farm, but more commonly it is stored in the rafters of a man's reception room or in the cooking hut, and issued to wives every few days for meals. Women prepare millet by grinding it into flour and cooking it with water as a porridge. It is also consumed as beer.

Sorghum

Sorghum produced on the bush farm is commonly interplanted with millet when the millet crop is weeded or thinned in early summer. Sorghum is occasionally sole planted on the bush farm if the stalks are to be used to stake a following yam crop. Sorghum is also rotated with maize on the compound farm.

Men contribute most of the labor to field preparation for sorghum by building the ridges on which sorghum is planted. Men are also responsible for most of the planting with some assistance from women. Planting is done by broadcasting the seed over the field with no subsequent turning of the soil.

Female/Male Labor Contribution to Sorghum Production

Crop	Field Prep.	Planting	Weeding	Harvesting	Processing	Storage
Sorghum	M	F: 20% M: 80%	F	F: 50% M: 50%	F	F

Women do all weeding for sorghum. Both men and women work on sorghum harvesting which, like millet, is done by having the men break down and cut the stalks while the women cut and bundle the heads of grain and carry them back to the compound. Sorghum intended for home consumption is stored unhusked on platforms until the rainy season, when it is stored inside in calabashes. Sorghum is an important cash crop for women in this region and surplus is traded, often in processed form. Sorghum may be processed in various ways. It can be ground into flour and cooked with water, and it is a preferred grain for making beer.

Cassava

Cassava has become an increasingly important crop in this region since early in this century because of its resistance to drought and its ability to grow in poor soils. It is important as a food crop, but as its significance as a cash crop has increased, so has men's involvement in its production. Cassava is the last crop in the bush/fallow cycle, but it is also interplanted with most other crops throughout the cycle, particularly with women's yams or on the compound farms.

Both men and women contribute to field preparation for cassava. Women's contribution is in clearing bush farms and compound farms on which cassava is interplanted while men's contribution is in building ridges.

Either men or women plant cassava that is grown alone, but women are responsible for planting cassava grown in yam fields or in the compound farm. Women do all the weeding. Cassava can be stored in the ground until it is needed for consumption or sale. It also stores well in its processed forms, as flour or gari; processing is a task performed by women.

Female/Male Labor Contribution to Cassava Production

Crop	Field Prep.	Planting	Weeding	Harvesting	Processing	Storage
Cassava	F: 25% M: 75%	F: 75% M: 25%	F	F: 75% M: 25%	F	F

Maize

Maize is grown in many different places on the Tiv farm. Most of it is grown on the compound farm where it is rotated with sorghum. It is also grown as a side crop in women's yam fields and it is occasionally grown in rice fields.

Women contribute to maize field preparation by clearing the yam and rice fields and preparing the compound farm. Men build the ridges in which the maize is planted. Maize grown in the yam fields or compound farm is planted and harvested by women while men share responsibility for maize in rice fields. Women weed all fields.

Maize is stored on the cob, frequently on the rafters of huts. It is processed by stewing it with other vegetables, making flour or boiling it on the cob.

Female/Male Labor Contribution to Maize Production

Crop	Field Prep.	Planting	Weeding	Harvesting	Processing	Storage
Maize	F: 25% M: 75%	F: 90% M: 10%	F	F: 90% M: 10%	F	F

Rice

Female/Male Labor Contribution to Rice Production

Crop	Field Prep.	Planting	Weeding	Harvesting	Processing	Storage
Rice	F: 10% M: 90%	F	F	F: 50% M: 50%	F: 50% M: 50%	F

Rice is important as both a food and a cash crop in this region. Once considered to be a women's crop, it has become an important cash crop for men over the past 30 years. Rice is grown on alluvial flood plains or irrigated areas near the main streams and rivers. These areas are generally not suitable for other crops so that rice is often grown in sole stands. Field preparation involves removing all weeds by hand, for which women are responsible, and building trenches and ridges, which men perform. Women plant the rice by dropping seeds into holes made with their big toe or by broadcasting the seed thinly. Women do all the weeding while men are responsible for the almost constant work on ditches, and repair of beds and ridges. Both women and men work together on harvesting and husking rice. At harvest, rice is tied into bundles and stacked in a central area for drying and threshing. Rice for the family's consumption is stored in palm baskets and surplus is sold as paddy immediately after harvest.

Benniseed

Female/Male Labor Contribution to Beniseed Production

Crop	Field Prep.	Planting	Weeding	Harvesting	Processing	Storage
Benni-seed	M	F: 50% M: 50%	F	F: 50% M: 50%	F	F

Benniseed was formerly an important cash crop in this region, produced to raise money for taxes. At present it is grown mainly for home consumption and local trade. When sole cropped, benniseed is planted on fallow land following the cassava rotation. It is frequently planted alone or interplanted with sorghum.

One of the advantages of benniseed production is that it requires relatively little labor. Field preparation is done by men. Both sexes plant the seed by broadcasting. Women do all weeding and both sexes work on the harvest. Benniseed is harvested by plucking and bundling the spikes and hanging them to dry. When thoroughly dry, the benniseed is pounded in a mortar and winnowed. It is stored in a woman's hut in large clay pots.

Watermelon

Watermelon is grown by the Tiv for its seeds, called "egusi" seeds. These are dried, dehusked and either ground for soup or chewed as a confectionery. Watermelons have become important as a cash crop in this region. Until recently most watermelon was grown on the compound farm, but as its cash value increased it began to replace the men's millet crop on the bush farm.

Watermelon seeds are planted in flat areas around the compound farm, which is prepared by women, or on the bush farm in ridges prepared by men. The rapid growth in the plant's groundcover reduces the need for weeding, which is done by women. Women harvest and process watermelon grown in the compound farm but men's role in harvesting is becoming more important as watermelon replaces their millet crop.

Female/Male Labor Contribution to Watermelon Production

Crop	Field Prep.	Planting	Weeding	Harvesting	Processing	Storage
Water-melon	F: 25% M: 75%	F: 25% M: 75%	F	F: 25% M: 75%	F	F

Cowpeas

The cowpea is a vegetable grown for its dried pea and for its fresh green leaves. Most of the cowpeas produced in this region are planted as a late crop and are interplanted with sorghum on the compound farm. Some early cowpeas may be interplanted with other vegetables on the sides of women's yam mounds. Except for mound building, women have primary responsibility for preparing the fields of the compound farm and contribute to preparation of yam fields. Women weed, harvest and process cowpeas; these are responsibilities that women hold for most of the fruits and vegetables that are grown or gathered on Tiv farms. Cowpeas are shelled by beating with sticks or breaking pods by hand. They are then soaked and washed to remove the outer skin. Dried cowpeas are stored in calabashes in women's huts.

Female/Male Labor Contribution to Cowpea Production

Crop	Field Prep.	Planting	Weeding	Harvesting	Processing	Storage
Cowpea	F: 25% M: 75%	F	F	F	F	F

APPENDIX III: NET RETURNS BY CROP

The chart below provides data on the net returns by crop of each of the crops targeted by the project. Net returns refers to the total net value of each crop, including both marketed and home-consumer production.

Calculations for net returns are based on price and yields projected by the project documents. Traditional pre-project refers to the net value of traditionally cultivated crops before the project. Improved post-project and traditional post-project refer to the value of a crop after the project. It is expected that after the project some proportion of each crop will continue to be cultivated using traditional methods while some proportion of each crop will be cultivated using the improved seeds and cultivation practices provided by the project.

APPENDIX III

NET RETURN BY CROP FOR TYPICAL 2.5 HECTARE FARM

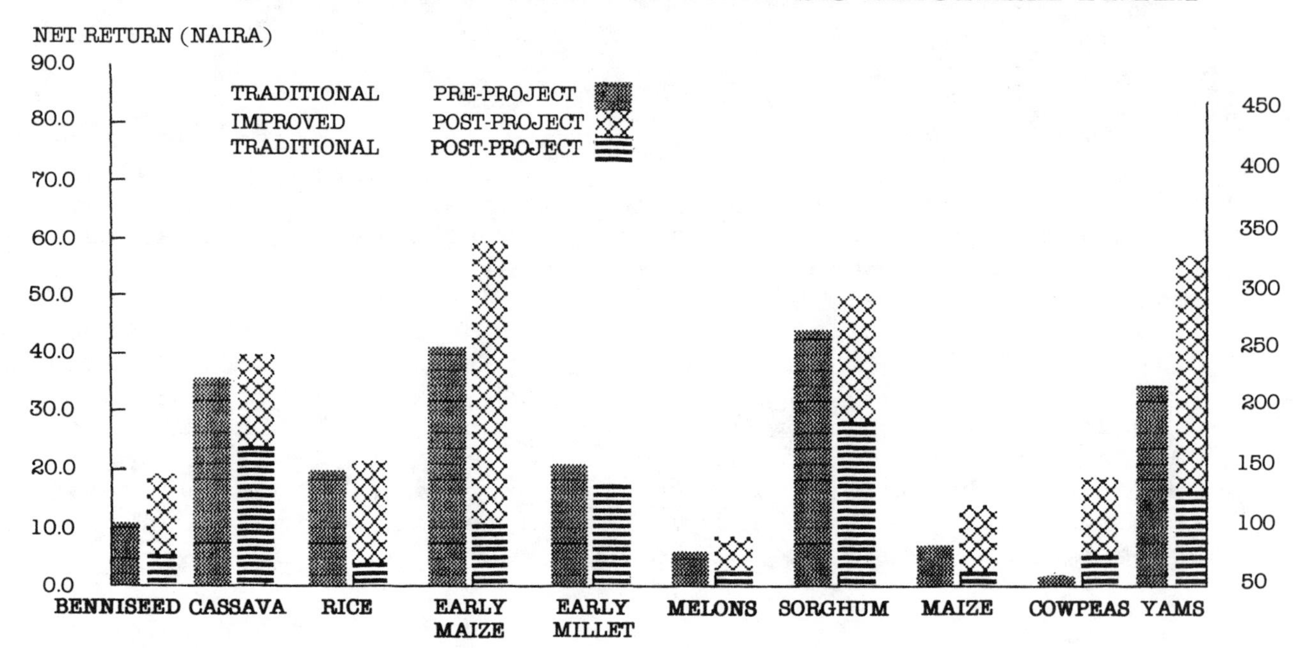

SOURCE: Project Documents

APPENDIX IV: FARM LABOR PROFILES BY CROP

The following charts show the farm labor profiles for the total farm, women and men from before and after the project, based on days spent on each crop. The number of person days per month in these profiles may differ slightly from the profiles in Chapter 4, which indicate person days spent on each crop activity. These differences are due to rounding errors.

APENDIX IV

CHART 1

TOTAL FARM LABOR PROFILE BY CROP (PRE-PROJECT)

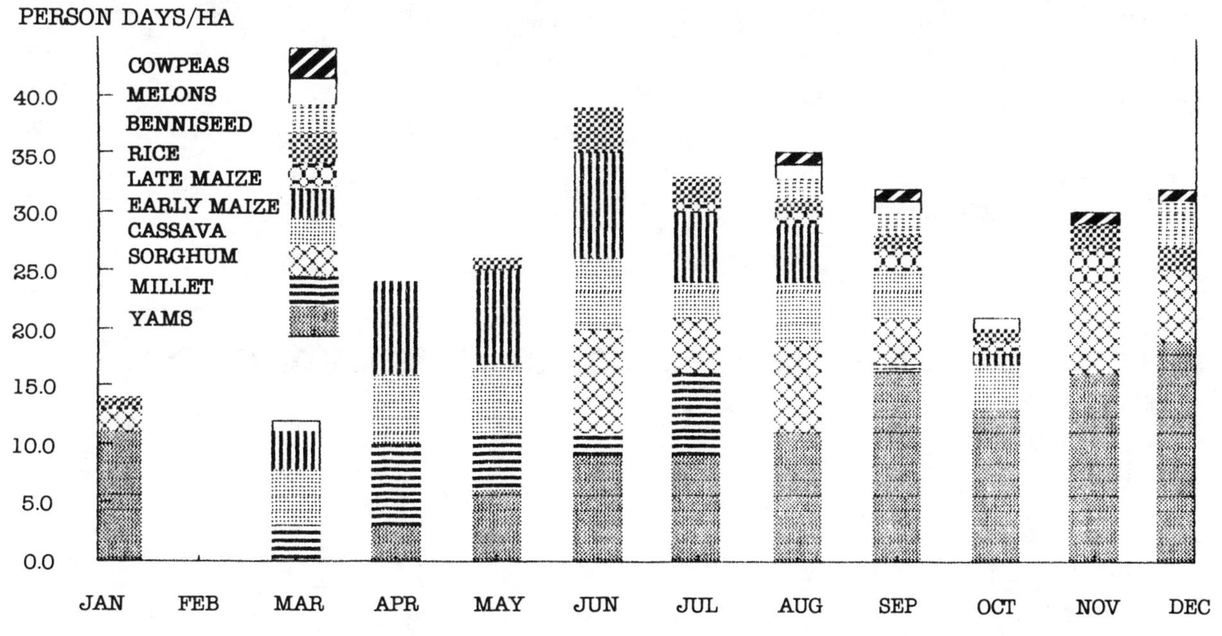

APENDIX IV

CHART 2
TOTAL FARM LABOR PROFILE BY CROP (POST-PROJECT)

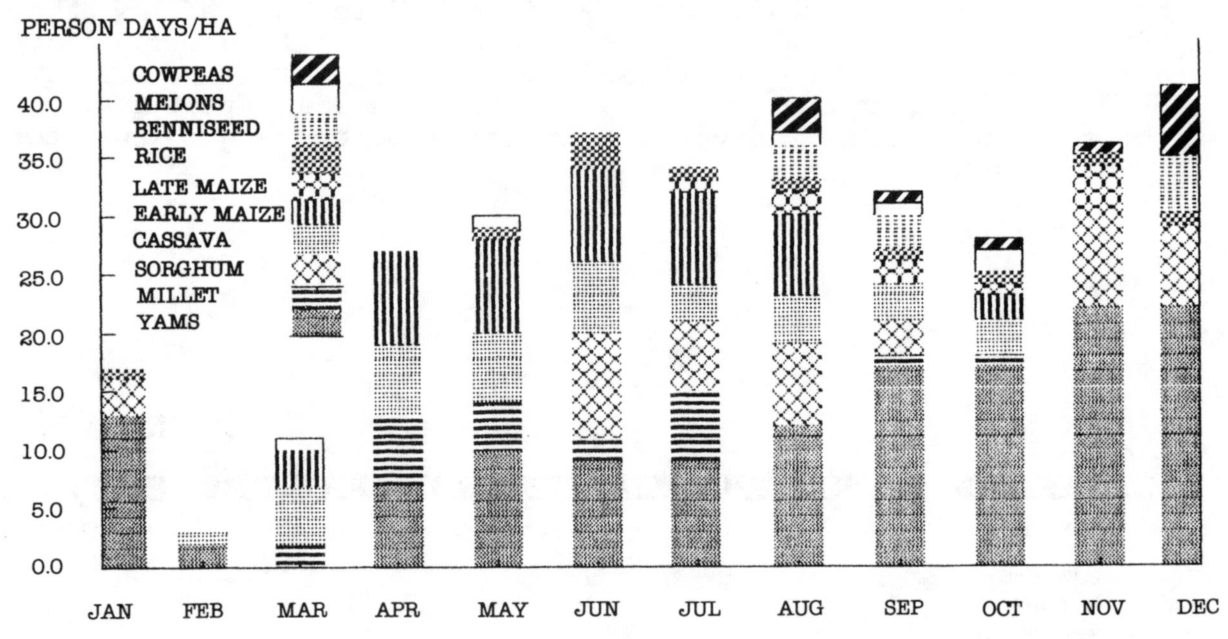

SOURCE: Project Documents

APENDIX IV

CHART 3
FEMALE LABOR PROFILE BY CROP (PRE-PROJECT)

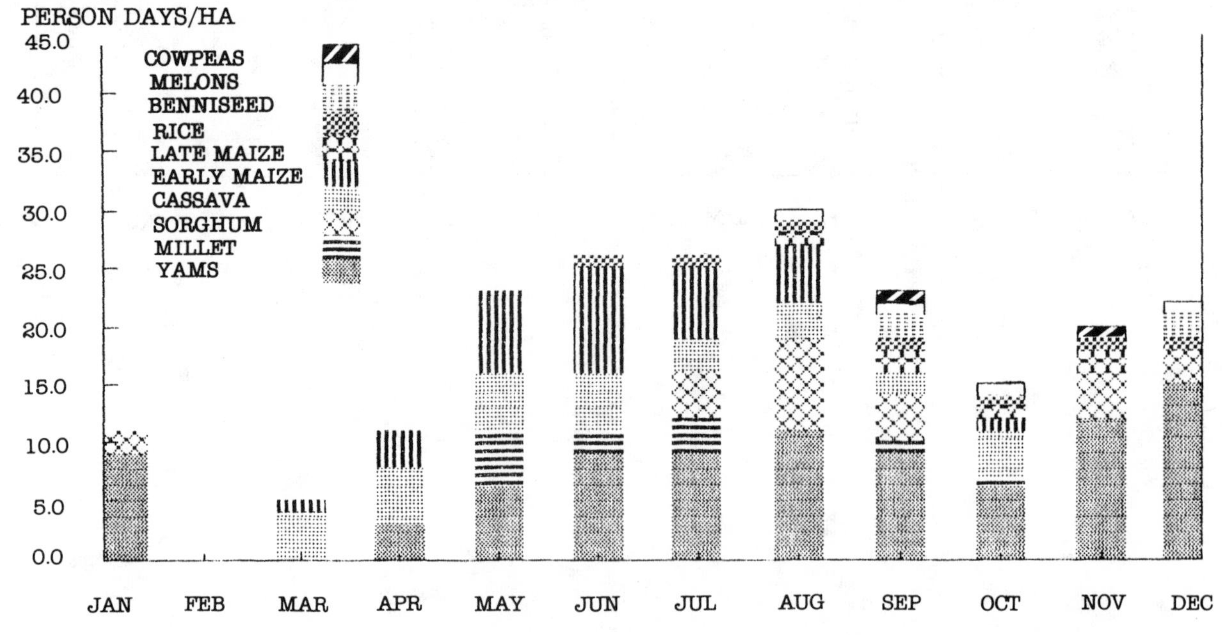

SOURCES: Bohannan and Bohannan, Tiv Economy; Vermeer, Agricultural and Dietary Practices Among the Tiv, Ibo and Birom Tribes, Nigeria; and Project Documents

APENDIX IV

CHART 4

FEMALE LABOR PROFILE BY CROP (POST-PROJECT)

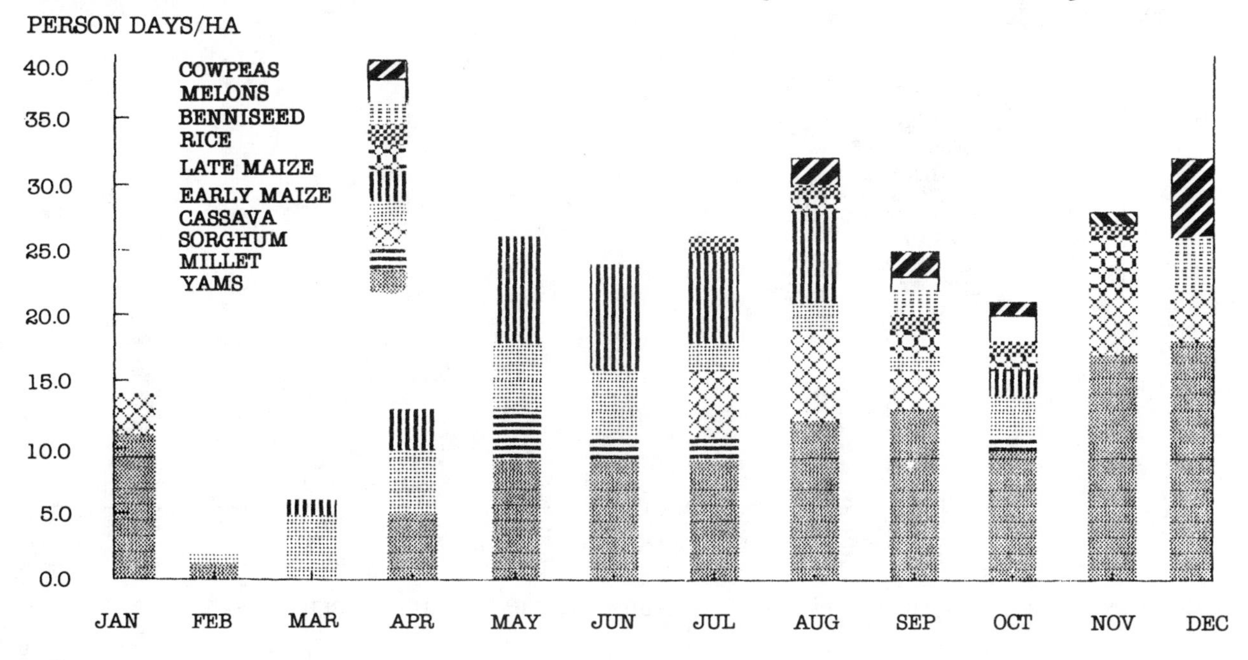

SOURCES: Bohannan and Bohannan, Tiv Economy; Vermeer, Agricultural and Dietary Practices Among the Tiv, Ibo and Birom Tribes, Nigeria; and Project Documents

APENDIX IV

CHART 5

MALE LABOR PROFILE BY CROP (PRE-PROJECT)

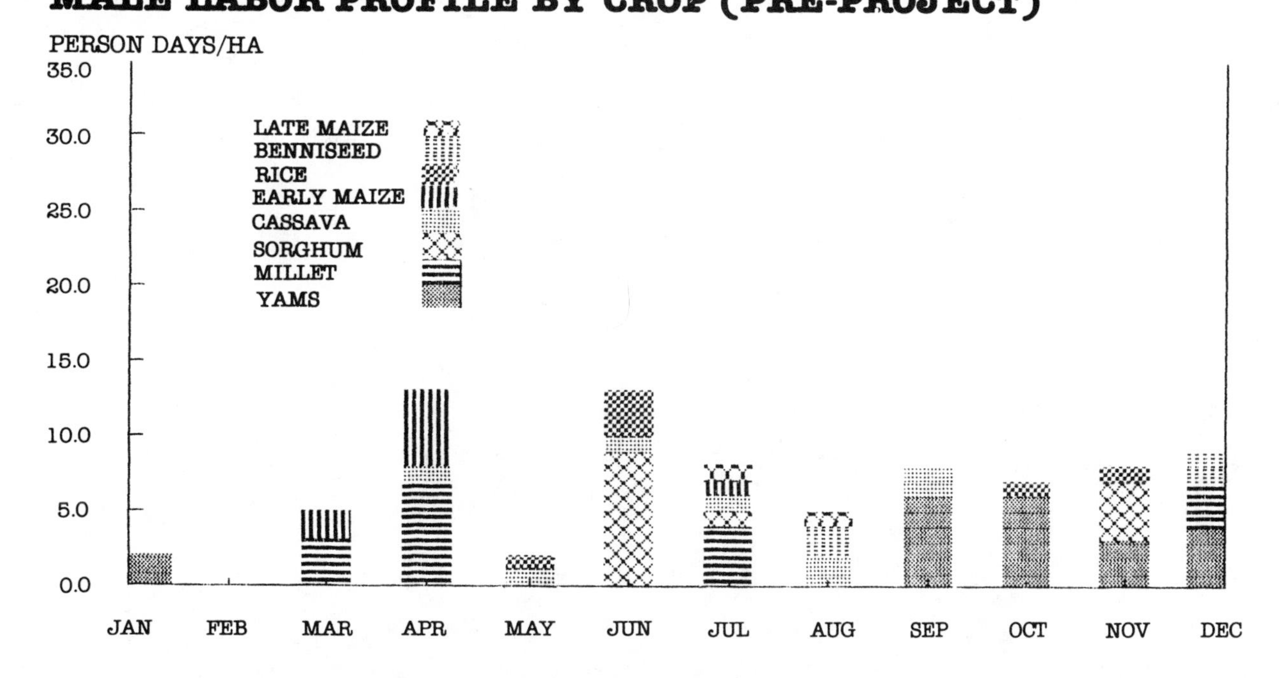

SOURCES: Bohannan and Bohannan, Tiv Economy; Vermeer, Agricultural and Dietary Practices Among the Tiv, Ibo and Birom Tribes, Nigeria; and Project Documents

CHART 6
MALE LABOR PROFILE BY CROP (POST-PROJECT)

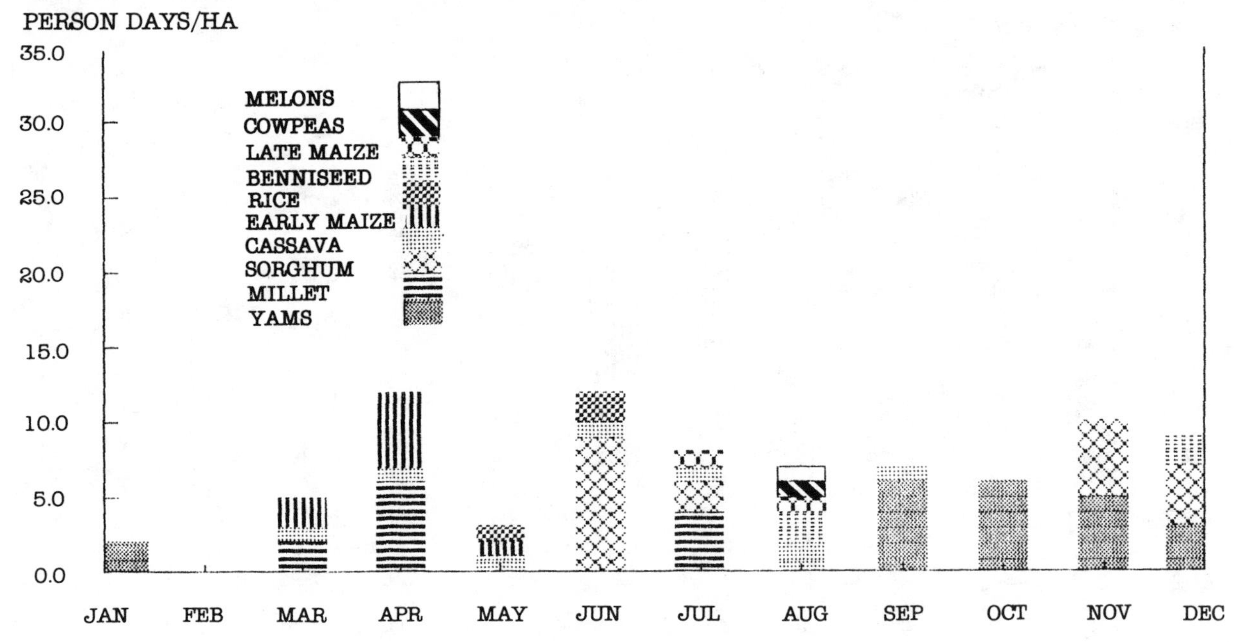

SOURCES: Bohannan and Bohannan, Tiv Economy; Vermeer, Agricultural and Dietary Practices Among the Tiv, Ibo and Birom Tribes, Nigeria; and Project Documents

BIBLIOGRAPHY

Abraham, R.C. *The Tiv People*. Farnborough Hunts, England: Gregg Press, 1968. Reprint of 1933 publication.

Adegeye, Adeduro. "The Commodity Board System for Food Crops: A New Dimension in Nigerian Agricultural Policy--A Comment," *Agricultural Administration*, Vol. 6, No. 3, 1979.

Adeyokunnu, Tomilayo. "Women and Agriculture in Nigeria." Department of Agricultural Economics, University of Ibadan, Ibadan, Nigeria, February 1980.

____________. "The Nigerian Rural Women: Some Policy Considerations for Development." Unpublished.

Ajaegbu, H.I. "Migrants and the Rural Economy in Nigeria," in Aderanti Adepoju, ed. *Internal Migration in Nigeria*. Institute of Population and Manpower Studies: University of Ife, Nigeria, 1976.

Akande, J.P. Debo. *Law and the Status of Women in Nigeria*. Addis Ababa: United Nations Economic Commission for Africa, African Training and Research Center for Women, 1979.

Apthorpe, Raymond. "Some Problems of Evaluation," in Carl Wistrand, ed. *Cooperatives and Rural Development in East Africa*. New York: African Publishing Corporation, 1970.

Awosika, Keziah. "Nigerian Women in the Informal Labor Market: Planning for Effective Participation." Paper presented to the Conference on Women and Development, Wellesley College, Boston, Massachusetts. June 2-6, 1976.

Baum, Warren. "The Project Cycle." *Finance and Development* December, 1978.

Bohannan, Laura. "Political Aspects of Tiv Social Organization," in John Middleton and David Tait, eds. *Tribes Without Rulers* London: Routledge and Kegan Paul, Ltd., 1958.

Bohannan, Paul. *Tiv Farm and Settlement*. London: Her Majesty's Stationery Office, 1954.

Bohannan, Paul and Laura Bohannan. *The Tiv of Central Nigeria*. London: International African Institute, 1969.

_______________. *Tiv Economy*. Evanston: Northwestern University Press, 1968.

Boserup, Ester. *Women's Role in Economic Development*. New York: St. Martin's Press, 1970.

Boulding, Elise. *Women in the Twentieth Century World*. New York: Sage, 1977.

Buvinic, Myra and Nadia Yousse. *Women-Headed Households: The Ignored Factor in Development Planning*. Department of State, Agency for International Development, 1978.

Cleave, John H. *African Farmers: Labor Use in the Development of Small-holder Agriculture*. New York: Praeger, 1974.

Cloud, Kathleen. *Sex Roles in Food Production and Food Distribution Systems in the Sahel*. Agency for International Development, December 15, 1977.

Christensen, Cheryl, et al. *Food Problems and Prospects in Sub-Saharan Africa: The Decade of the 1980's*. U.S. Department of Agriculture, FAER No. 166. 1981.

DeWilde, John C. *Experiences with Agricultural Development in Tropical Africa*. Two volumes. Baltimore: Johns Hopkins Press, 1967.

Dixon, Ruth. *Assessing the Impact of Development Projects on Women*. AID Program Evaluation Discussion Paper No. 8. Office of Women in Development and Office of Evaluation, U.S. Agency for International Development. Washington, D.C. 1980.

Hafkin, Nancy and Edna Bay, eds. *Women in Africa: Studies in Social and Economic Change*. Stanford University Press, 1976.

Hill, Polly. "Hidden Trade in Hausaland," *Man* Vol. 4, No. 3, Sept. 1969.

Ike, D.N. "Land Tenure Practices in Nigeria," *The American Journal of Economics and Sociology*. Vol. 36, No. 2, April, 1977.

International Center for Research on Women. *Keeping Women Out: A Structural Analysis for Women's Employment in Developing Countries*. April, 1980.

Janelid, Ingrid. *The Role of Women in Nigerian Agriculture*. Rome: Food and Agriculture Organization, May 1975.

Longhurst, Richard. *Rural Development Planning and the Sexual Division of Labor: A Case Study of a Moslem Hausa Village in Northern Nigeria*. Geneva: ILO, 1980.

McSweeney, Brenda. "Collection and Analysis of Data on Rural Women's Time Use," in Sandra Zeidenstein, ed. *Studies in Family Planning: Learning About Rural Women*. Vol. 10, Nos. 11 and 12, November/December 1979.

National Council of Women Societies of Nigeria. "Laws and Customs Affecting Women." Paper prepared for National Seminar on Women in Rural Development: Women in Rural Areas of Nigeria, Benin City, Nigeria, June 13-15, 1979.

Norman, D.W., David Pryor, and Christopher Gibbs. *Technical Change and the Small Farmer in Hausaland, Northern Nigeria*. Michigan State University. Africa Rural Economy Paper No. 21, 1979.

Okonjo, Kamene. "Rural Women's Credit System: A Nigerian Example" in Sondra Zeidenstein, ed. *Studies in Family Planning: Learning about Rural Women*. Vol. 10, Nos. 11 and 12, November/December 1979.

Patel, A.U., and Anthonio, Q.B. "Farmers' Wives in Agricultural Development: The Nigerian Case." University of Ibadan, Nigeria. Paper prepared for the 15th International Congress of Agricultural Economics, Sao Paulo, Brazil, August 1973.

Rogers, Barbara. *The Domestication of Women*. New York: St. Martin's Press, 1979.

Salau, Ademola T. "Land Policies for Urban and National Development in Nigeria". *Journal of Administration Overseas*, Vol. 17, No. 3, 1978.

Staudt, Kathleen. "Development Interventions and Differential Technology Impact Between Men and Women." Paper Presented at the Third World Conference, University of Nebraska at Omaha, October 24-27, 1979.

Sweet, Donald, et al. *A Seven Country Survey on the Roles of Women in Rural Development*. Washington, D.C. 1974.

United Nations. Department of Economic and Social Affairs. *Report to the Interregional Meeting of Experts on the Integration of Women in Development*. New York, June 19-28, 1972. New York, 1973. ST/SOA/120.

United Nations Economic Commission for Africa, Human Resources Development Division. "Women: The Neglected Human Resources for African Development," *Canadian Journal of African Studies*, Vol. 6, No. 2, 1972.

Vermeer, Donald. "Agricultural and Dietary Practices Among the Tiv, Ibo, and Birom Tribes, Nigeria." Ph. D. dissertation, University of California, Berkeley, 1964.

_______________. "The Tradition of Experimentation in Swidden Cultivation Among the Tiv of Nigeria," in John W. Frazier and Bart Fostein, eds. *Applied Geography Conference*. Vol. 2, SUNY-Binghamton, 1979.

_______________. "Population Pressure and Crop Rotational Change Among the Tiv of Nigeria," *Annals of the Association of American Geographers*. Vol. 60, No. 2, June 1979.

Wallace, J.G. "The Tiv System of Election," *Journal of African Administration*. Vol. 10, No. 2, April 1958.

Weidemann, Celia Jean. "Case Studies of Five Rural Families in Eastern Nigeria: Implications for Planning Home Economics Extension Programmes," *Home Economics Research Bulletin*. No. 1, May, 1977. Federal Department of Agriculture, Ibadan, Nigeria.

World Bank. Various project papers and documents.

World Federation of Mental Health. "The Tiv of Nigeria," in Margaret Mead, ed. *Cultural Patterns and Technical Change*. New York: UNESCO, 1955.

Zuckerman, Paul S. "Some Characteristics of Nigerian Smallholders: A Case Study from Western Nigeria," *African Study Review*. Vol. 23, No. 3, December 1979.

ALSO AVAILABLE FROM KUMARIAN PRESS

Women's Roles and Gender Differences in Development: Cases for Planners
Prepared by the Population Council.

The Nemow Case, by Ingrid Palmer
February 1985 $6.75 ISBN: 0-931816-16-5

Sex Roles in the Nigerian Tiv Farm Household, by Mary E. Burfisher and Nadine R. Horenstein
February 1985 $6.75 ISBN: 0-931816-17-3

Agricultural Policy Implementation: A Case Study from Western Kenya, by Kathleen Staudt
February 1985 $6.75 ISBN: 0-931816-18-1

Kano River Irrigation Project, by Cecilia Jackson
Pub. date July 1985 $6.75

The Ilora Farm Settlement in Nigeria, by Heather Spiro
Pub. date July 1985 $6.75

The Impact of Agrarian Reform on Women, by Ingrid Palmer
Pub. date July 1985 $6.75

The Impact of Male Out-Migration on Women in Farming, by Ingrid Palmer
Pub. date July 1985 $6.75

Kumarian Press offers a discount on purchases of full sets of these volumes. For more information, to ask for our catalog or to place an order, write or call

KUMARIAN PRESS
630 Oakwood Avenue, Suite 119
West Hartford, CT 06110
(203) 524-0214